THE COLLAGE WORKBOOK

THE COLLAGE WORKBOOK

HOW TO GET STARTED AND STAY INSPIRED

RANDEL PLOWMAN

LARK CRAFTS

Asheville

Editor:
Kathleen McCafferty

Art Director:
Travis Medford

Photographer:
Nicholas Wynia

Illustrator:
Orrin Lundgren

Cover Designer:
Travis Medford

DEDICATION:

This book is dedicated to Stacy, for all of her loving support, and also to Simone, the greatest artist I know.

LARK CRAFTS

An Imprint of Sterling Publishing
387 Park Avenue South
New York, NY 10016

If you have questions or comments about
this book, please visit: larkcrafts.com

Library of Congress Cataloging-in-Publication Data

Plowman, Randel.
  The collage workbook : how to get started & stay inspired / Randel Plowman.
      p. cm.
  Includes index.
  ISBN 978-1-4547-0199-6 (pb-trade pbk. : alk. paper)
  1. Collage--Technique. I. Title.
  TT910.P59 2012
  702.81'2--dc23
                      2011030969

10 9 8 7 6 5 4 3

Published by Lark Crafts
An Imprint of Sterling Publishing Co., Inc.
387 Park Avenue South, New York, NY 10016

Text © 2012, Randel Plowman
Photography © 2012, Lark Crafts, an Imprint of Sterling Publishing Co., Inc.
Illustrations © 2012, Lark Crafts, an Imprint of Sterling Publishing Co., Inc.

Distributed in Canada by Sterling Publishing,
c/o Canadian Manda Group, 165 Dufferin Street
Toronto, Ontario, Canada M6K 3H6

Distributed in the United Kingdom by GMC Distribution Services,
Castle Place, 166 High Street, Lewes, East Sussex, England BN7 1XU

Distributed in Australia by Capricorn Link (Australia) Pty Ltd.,
P.O. Box 704, Windsor, NSW 2756 Australia

Manufactured in China

ISBN 13: 978-1-4547-0199-6

For information about custom editions, special sales, premium and corporate purchases, please contact Sterling Special Sales Department at 800-805-5489 or specialsales@sterlingpub.com.

For information about desk and examination copies available to college and university professors, requests must be submitted to academic@larkbooks.com. Our complete policy can be found at www.larkcrafts.com.

CONTENTS

INTRODUCTION

This book is the result of almost 30 years of exploring the world of collage. It started out innocently enough: I was taking a two-dimensional design class at the local university. One of the final projects was to make a collage using the basic elements of design. My professor brought in huge boxes of stuff—wallpaper books, assorted old magazines, and stacks of vintage ephemera. The excitement I felt was incredible—I quickly busied myself digging through the piles and giddily selected the items that spoke to me.

After that, I was hooked. I've been making collages ever since, including daily collages that I've been posting on my blog, A Collage A Day (www.acollageaday.com) for the last six years. Even now, I *still* get excited about making collage for the simple reason that I get to collect things I love, and I get to use those things to make art. Collage is inexpensive—all you need is some glue, a pair of scissors, and some imagery that you like. With a basic understanding of design, anyone can do it.

When I set out to write *The Collage Workbook*, I wanted to share my enthusiasm for the art of collage with you, including all the tools and techniques I know. I also wanted to create a unique experience to get you going. That's why you'll find **50 CREATIVITY EXERCISES** (starting on page 46), where you can jump right in, start experimenting, and get inspired. And while I can't present you with a huge box of "stuff," like my professor did for me, I've included an **IMAGE LIBRARY** in the back of the book (page 116) filled with copyright-free imagery that you can copy, clip, and use as you wish. Visit my website at www.acollageaday.com for links to digital downloads of these images.

Of course, you'll probably want to collect imagery that's meaningful to you as well. Gathering images is an important aspect of collage making and the materials you choose make your collages one-of-a-kind. I offer many different ideas for finding imagery (pages 19 to 21), including digital resources you'll want to explore.

Often, it's the story behind the ephemera that's most compelling. You can imagine the child that scribbled over the faces of their storybook, the student whose name remains decades later written in pencil inside their textbook, and the person who crafted endearing letters in beautiful script. Collagists are drawn to the artifacts of time, and how these items—and these people—connect to our lives.

In the end, collage is really the art of "listening" to your materials. If you stay open, you'll surprise yourself with what emerges. I hope that with *The Collage Workbook* as your guide you'll be filled with a sense of discovery. I'd love to see what you create with some of the ideas from this book, and invite you to share your collages at www.acollageaday.com.

Randel Plowman

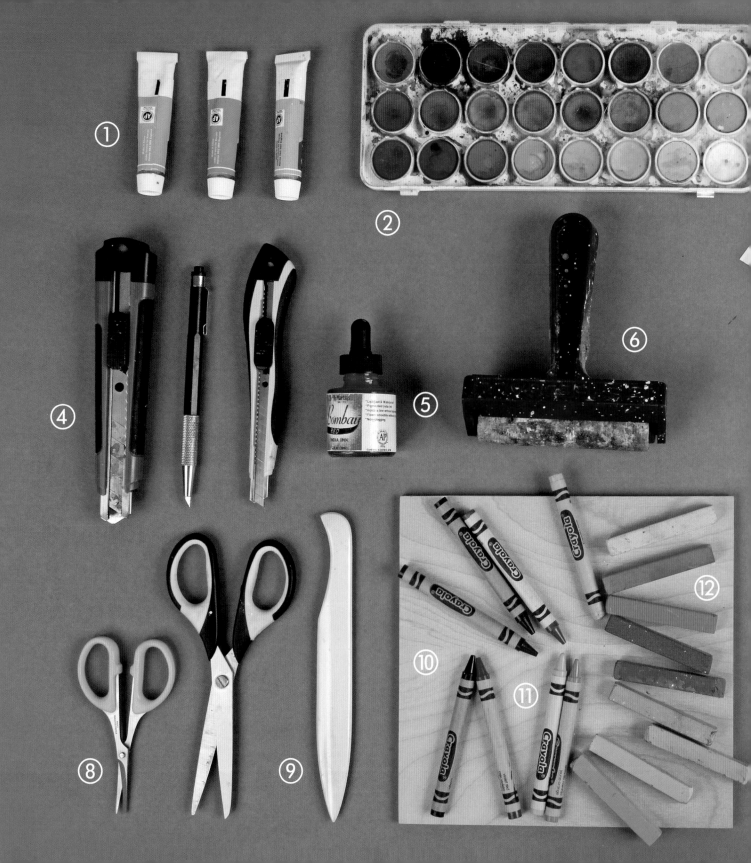

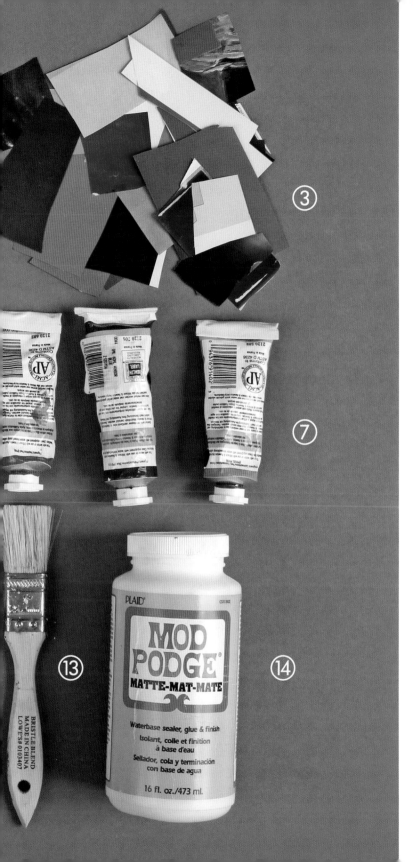

BASIC TOOL KIT

Here are some of the basic tools and materials you'll want to gather for your own collage-making adventures. Of course the materials you use are ultimately up to you, but these are some of the essential supplies I like to use. In the pages that follow, I'll discuss each one in depth, as well as some additional materials you might like to try. You probably already have some of these supplies at home, and you can find all of them at your local art supply store.

① Gouache paints (page 16)

② Watercolor paint (page 16)

③ Scraps of colored paper and imagery (page 20)

④ Utility and craft knives (page 15)

⑤ India ink (page 16)

⑥ Brayer (page 18)

⑦ Acrylic paint (page 16)

⑧ Small fine-tip and all-purpose scissors (page 15)

⑨ Bone folder (page 18)

⑩ Plywood support (page 12). Mat board, cardboard and watercolor paper work great too.

⑪ Crayons (page 17)

⑫ Pastels (page 17)

⑬ Medium-size bristle brush (page 17)

⑭ White glue (page 13)

TOOLS & MATERIALS

SUPPORTS

Supports, also known as substrates, are the foundation on which you'll build your collage. You'll want to select a support that can handle the layers of glue, imagery, and color mediums that you plan to use in your collage. Supports can vary from watercolor paper and heavy mat board to plywood or even canvas.

Watercolor papers come in various sizes and are sold in both sheets and pads. It's available in two varieties: hot press, which has a smooth surface, and cold press, which has a rough, textured surface. Watercolor paper is also produced in various weights or thicknesses, numbered in either pounds (lbs) per ream or grams per square meter (gsm). The most common type is 90 lb (200 gsm), 140 lb (300 gsm), and 300 lb (about 620 gsm). It looks and feels a bit like blotting paper. I personally use an archival 140 lb cold press watercolor paper as a support for most of my collages.

Mat board is available in a range of sizes and thicknesses. It provides good support for heavier materials, such as leather, vinyl, and lightweight three-dimensional objects.

Davey board is most commonly used in bookmaking and is a very rigid substrate that works well for heavier materials.

Cardboard can be found in various forms, sizes, and thicknesses and is readily available, especially in the form of recycled boxes.

Bristol board is an uncoated, machine-finished paperboard available in sheets and pads. I like to use it for photomontages.

Painting panels are made from high-density fiber core and plywood, and engineered for stability. They can be found mounted on wooden frame strips, and unmounted, and are available in an assortment of sizes, both primed and unprimed. I recommend coating unprimed panels with gesso to help give them a little tooth. Otherwise, they're very porous.

Plywood can be found in various thicknesses, including ¼-inch (6 mm), ½-inch (1.3 cm), and ¾-inch (1.9 cm) sizes. Plywood is also available in 4 x 8-foot (1.2 x 2.7 m), 4 x 4-foot (1.2 x 1.2 m), 2 x 4-foot (61 x 122 cm), and 2 x 2-foot (61 x 61 cm) sheets. It offers excellent support for gluing heavy objects to it.

Hardboard is found in both ⅛-inch (3 mm) and ¼-inch (6 mm) thicknesses. It's made of steamed and compressed wood fiber and works well if you're gluing heavier objects.

Canvas can be found either stretched on frames, glued to panels, or in sheets. For convenience, I recommend purchasing stretched canvas or canvas panels unless you're comfortable mounting it to a surface yourself.

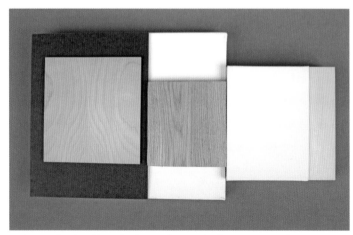

Left to right: hardboard, plywood, stretched canvas, wood shelving, foam board, painting panel

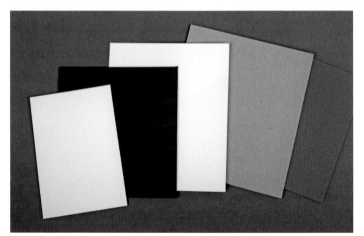

Left to right: canvas painting panel, mat board, white cardboard, davey board, cardboard

ADHESIVES

There are many different kinds of glue available on the market today. In my studio, I typically use one or two glues and a couple of different mediums to protect my collages. In any case, you'll want to consider the best glue for the job: the heavier the materials you are gluing to the support, the stronger and thicker the adhesive should be. If using lighter materials, you'll want to use thinner adhesive.

White Glues

MOD PODGE is my primary glue. You can find it in gloss and matte finishes, and in archival and non-archival versions. It has a smooth consistency, and can be used as a glue, sealer, and protectant. It's a wonderful glue for applying surface decorations, as in the case of decoupage.

POLYVINYL ACETATE GLUE (PVA) is the same consistency as Mod Podge. It's a good all-purpose glue, but it's not archival. You can find different brands of archival PVA glue, which is typically used for bookmaking.

Paste-Type Adhesives

YES! PASTE is archival (acid-free) and can be thinned with water.

PERMANENT GLUE STICKS dry clear and wrinkle-free, and are available in acid-free varieties. These are great for adhering thinner materials and for working up quick collages.

METHYL CELLULOSE ADHESIVE, when dissolved in water, produces a liquid adhesive, which has a neutral pH.

WHEAT PASTE comes in powder form; all you have to do is add cold water and stir. It works especially well with porous paper and is great for large-scale collages.

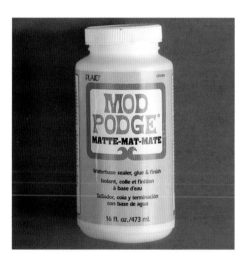
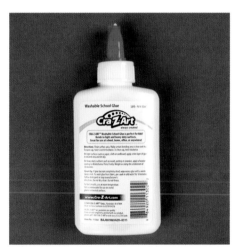
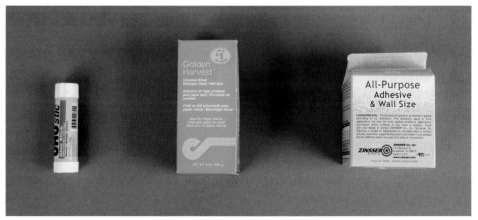

Top, left to right: two types of white glue; bottom, left to right: glue stick, wheat paste, wallpaper adhesive

Acrylic Mediums

Acrylic mediums serve many purposes: they can be used as a glue, a finish, and a transfer medium.

MATTE MEDIUM is a very good adhesive for thin papers, such as tracing and tissue papers. It can also be added to acrylic paint for a matte finish. GLOSS MEDIUM functions in the same way, but provides a glossy, shiny finish.

GELS are available in both gloss and matte finishes. They are thicker than matte and gloss mediums and work really well for collage and decoupage.

MODELING PASTE is a mixture of ground marble and resin. It dries hard, like cement, and can be sanded. Modeling paste works well when using hardboard as a substrate.

Protectants

Protectants offer the final touch to coat and seal your finished collages.

GLOSS AND MATTE MEDIUM varieties will protect your completed collages; choose the kind of finish that appeals to you.

UV-RESISTANT CLEAR SPRAY protects against harmful ultraviolet light and is available in gloss and matte finishes. It creates a clear moisture barrier and is acid-free and archival.

Rubber-Based Adhesives

MULTIPURPOSE SPRAY ADHESIVE has high coverage and high tack. Take care not to overspray lightweight images or the ends may curl.

PAPER CEMENT does not shrink or wrinkle the paper when it's applied. Some brands are acid-free.

RUBBER CEMENT is a fluid adhesive made from elastic (latex) polymers mixed in solvent. It is not archival.

Top, left to right: gloss medium, matte medium; bottom, left to right: rubber cement, multipurpose spray adhesive, paper cement

CUTTING TOOLS

There are a wide variety of scissors and other cutting tools for collage making. You can use whatever you have at home to get started, but you may want to invest in some small or decorative-edge scissors as your collage work progresses.

Scissors

HEAVY-DUTY SCISSORS are the best choice for cutting heavier materials, such as leather, cardboard, and aluminum.

You're bound to already have a pair of GENERAL-PURPOSE SCISSORS at home. They're available in a wide variety of styles, including pairs made especially for left-handed users.

FINE-TIP SCISSORS work well when cutting very detailed, fine imagery.

DECORATIVE-EDGE SCISSORS are available in an assortment of designs and can be found in the scrapbooking aisle of your arts and crafts supply store.

Knives

LARGE UTILITY KNIVES are the best choice for cutting heavy materials that require a perfectly straight edge.

MEDIUM-WEIGHT RETRACTABLE KNIVES serve a good all-purpose function and work particularly well with cardboard.

CRAFT KNIVES are pencil-like knives used for precision cutting.

CIRCLE CUTTERS are easy, no-fuss tools for cutting perfect circles of varying sizes.

ROTARY CUTTERS are a good choice for cutting straight lines in fabric.

DESKTOP PAPER CUTTERS are available in both blade and rotary designs and work well for quick, efficient cutting. Depending on the model, you can even cut more than one piece of a paper at a time.

Cutting Mats

SELF-SEALING CUTTING MATS are indispensable when using rotary blades and straight utility blades. Cutting mats provide a long-lasting surface that can be cut without showing marks or cutting lines. They are available in various sizes and most come printed with handy ruler and guidelines for 45° and 60° angles.

Top, left to right: scissors, cutting mats; bottom, left to right: knives, desktop paper cutter

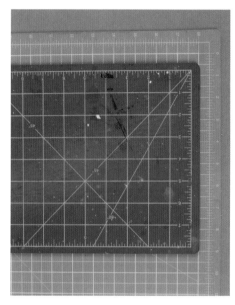

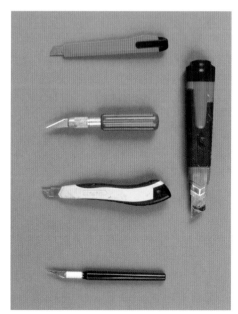

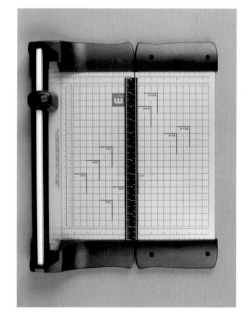

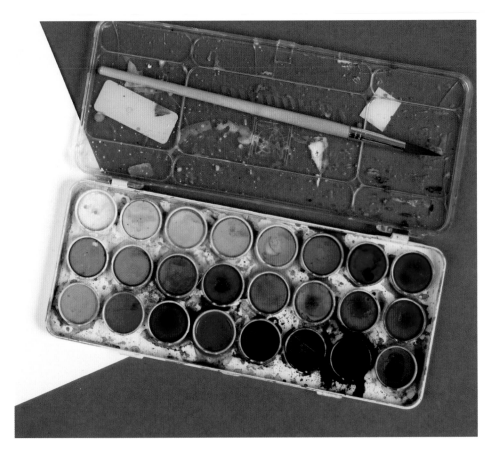

PAINTING MEDIUMS

Watercolor paints are available in both tubes and pans and are perfect for adding transparent color to paper and other materials.

Gouache is, personally, my favorite paint to use. I enjoy the velvety matte characteristic that these paints offer. Gouache can be used as either a transparent or an opaque paint and can be thinned with water.

Acrylic paints are versatile, water-based paints that work wonderfully for collage. Acrylic paints dry quickly and can even be painted over when dry. You can also add both matte and gloss mediums (page 14) to create a variety of surfaces and add modeling paste (page 14) to create textures.

India ink can be found in a variety of colors and diluted with water to create a transparent wash.

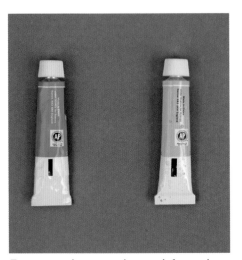

Top: watercolor paints; bottom, left to right: gouache, acrylic paints, India ink

BRUSHES

Soft sable brushes are great for watercolor, gouache, and India ink, and for applying thinner glue mediums and protectants. **Bristle paintbrushes** have stiff bristles and work well for acrylic paints and most glues. They're available in various sizes, including both round and flat heads.

DRAWING MEDIUMS

I find myself using **crayons** more and more. They work great for adding quick color and can create interesting textures when watercolor or India ink is applied over them.

Water-soluble crayons and pencils are available in a variety of brands. When water is added to the surface of the paper, the line or mark created with these mediums turns to watercolor. My personal favorite to use is Caran d'Ache Neocolor II Aquarelle.

Pencils and pens come in a wide assortment, including graphite, charcoal, markers, and pens with different tips to achieve different line thicknesses.

Pastels are available in both chalk and oil form and can be found in an array of colors. Chalk pastels should be set using a fixative. To create a wash for oil pastels, you can combine them with mineral spirits or turpentine.

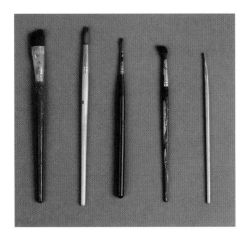

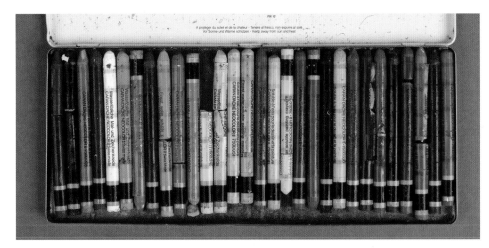

Top, left to right: brushes, crayons; center: water-soluble crayons; bottom, left to right: pens and pencils, pastels

FLATTENING TOOLS

Printmaking brayers and **wallpaper seam rollers** are wonderful for preventing glued paper from wrinkling when you apply it to your substrate. They also help keep the layers of your collage flat. Look for brayers that are made of hard rubber or plastic. Seam rollers can be found in your local hardware or paint store.

Bone folders are also useful for flattening your image and when working with transfers. When choosing a bone folder avoid the cheap plastic ones. Purchase a bone folder that is made of real bone; they are easier to clean and will last a lifetime.

Safety glass can be used to help flatten collages that are already finished. Sandwich your collage between several layers of safety glass overnight to flatten it.

You can also make a simple press to flatten your collages at home. See the instructions on page 45 for how to make your own simple press.

Left to right: bone folders, brayers

HARDWARE & SOFTWARE

Today's collagist can access and manipulate images with the help of computer hardware and software tools. Although not necessary for collage making, these tools present a host of opportunities for controlling imagery and creating the exact results you want in your finished work. And when it comes to creating image transfers, they're essential.

These days, most homes are equipped with a computer and most libraries and print or copy shops have labs that can be accessed. In addition to finding and downloading online imagery, you can manipulate the imagery you find using with image-editing software like Photoshop, Adobe Illustrator, and Paint

Shop Pro. Some programs, like Picasa, can be downloaded for free online. Although not necessary for your collage practice, these tools are invaluable for altering imagery with regard to orientation, size, resolution, and many other functions.

Simple ink-jet printers are good for printing on tracing and other kinds of paper and can be found inexpensively at home and office supply stores. If investing in one for your home studio or office, look for printers that use pigmented ink, not dye-based inks. Pigmented ink will transfer, whereas dye-based ink will not. Paper typically doesn't absorb pigmented ink, which sits on top of the fibers in small, encapsulated particles; dye-based ink is absorbed into the paper's fibers. This is why pigmented ink works better for transfers (see page 40).

Laser printers work well for general printing and can also be used to create transfers. See page 38 for steps to create laser transfers using tracing paper.

Scanners are great for scanning precious imagery like vintage photos or images in old books or magazines that you can't bring yourself to cut up and use in your work. They're also handy for preserving digital files of your completed collages. For a fun idea to create a no-glue collage, check out the Scan Only creativity exercise on page 92.

GETTING STARTED

GATHERING IMAGERY

Collecting imagery and other materials for collage making can be as exciting as making the collage itself. I've always been a collector of things, finding myself drawn to the secret life of things as I move through the world. It doesn't matter if I'm walking down the street, taking out the trash, eating breakfast at a diner, or visiting a secondhand store. The littlest thing can speak to me with such significance. What we look for and collect as collage artists makes our work uniquely our own.

To jump right in, you can turn to the Image Library on page 116 and see what sparks your imagination. For a digital download of these images, you can also visit my website at www.acollageaday. com. For materials with a particular sense of time and history, you'll want to dig a little deeper. Here are some suggestions for gleaning imagery in your town.

Start at home. When making personal collages, you don't have to go any farther than your own house. Collage making is a great opportunity to see what you've got stashed away at home. Dig through nostalgic items like old letters and photographs and see what's there. You can always scan and print these items out instead of using the originals. And then there are newspapers, magazines, catalogs, and books to look through. Don't forget to rummage through your recycling bin, too, and consider using decorative stationary, wrapping paper, tissue paper, and even brown paper bags that you have lying around.

Secondhand stores are a great resource for finding materials to use in your work. I have a few that I frequent on a daily basis. You never know what you'll find. You may want to start with the books, but don't overlook unpacked boxes, old photo albums, stacks of records, and other nooks and crannies where visual treasures like to hide. The same goes for flea markets. Roll up your sleeves and dig around to see what you can find.

Libraries can be a great place to source ephemera. I used to live within a few blocks of a local public library. Every month they would have a used book sale. Often, my favorite books were the ones that were free. They were especially worn and showed signs of age—perfect for collage. Many were no longer in circulation or were outdated school-books. (See page 70 for some examples of the work I created using these books.) Of course, it goes without saying, but you can always check out any book you like with the intention of scanning imagery, too. Just keep your scissors away from the books you have to return.

Daily walks around your neighborhood can yield surprising results. Take a minute to pick up that receipt or crumpled note, scrap of packaging, intriguing to-do list, or discarded doodle. You'll help beautify your neighborhood and you might just find the perfect piece to activate your next collage. Take a look at a collage I created in just this way on page 77.

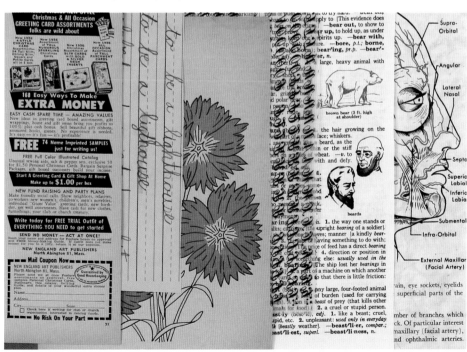

DECORATIVE PAPERS

From wrapping paper, patterned scrapbooking paper, pages of old books, handwritten notes, tissue paper, wallpaper, and the newspapers, magazines, and food packages at the bottom of your recycling bin, you can find all kinds of decorative papers to add to your collage work.

In my own work, I use tracing paper to create transparent layers, and for image transfer. You can hand color it as you desire, or you can cut pieces of colored tissue paper and superimpose those to create additional, sheer layers. See page 74 for some examples of this.

I also enjoy printing on everyday paper, such as lined composition paper, yellow legal paper, graph paper, and ledger paper. There's something visually interesting about combining the familiar with the found. Placing everyday "working" papers in artistic compositions gives them new meaning. Use your own pieces of everyday paper, or turn to the Image Library on page 116 for some ready-to-use samples for your work.

FINDING IMAGERY ONLINE

The Internet offers a wealth of information and imagery that's ripe for picking, but take care to seek out works that are copyright-free. Use your best judgment. It might not matter as much for collage work that you keep in a personal journal, but should you decide to scan those personal collages and put them online for all to see, or try to sell your work, you'll want to be more discerning.

To be safe, you can always search for royalty-free clip art and copyright-free images to use in your work. There are also a number of books and software CD-ROM titles that feature copyright-free clip and line art. The subject matter can range from historic designs, ornamental borders, and floral images to animals, birds, and people. Online, you can browse the following sites to inspire you in your collage journey, but for each case consider the intended use and assess the copyright status of any image before helping yourself.

Online Image Sources

Library of Congress Image Database
www.loc.gov/pictures

This site offers literally thousands of images that can be downloaded from their digital collection, with notes on restrictions and copyright use. It includes amazing artwork, old photographs, and even historic American building surveys and landscapes. Search for your hometown and see what comes up.

Library of Congress' Flickr Photostream
www.flickr.com/photos/library_of_congress

This collection is a wonderful resource for vintage photographs and features work with no known copyright restrictions. See images from the turn of the nineteenth century and beyond, including soldiers from the Civil War, the jazz greats of the 1930s and '40s, newspaper illustrations from the beginning of the twentieth century, and more.

Reusable Art
www.reusableart.com

All of the images in this collection are copyright-free in the United States and any country that extends copyrights up to seventy years after the death of the original artist, making them in the public domain and free to use. You'll find a host of interesting images that have been rescued from old books, magazines, and other print materials.

Karen's Whimsy
http://karenswhimsy.com/public-domain-images/

This site offers a collection of hundreds of free images from the founder's personal collection of old books, magazines, and postcards, all printed prior to 1923 and in the public domain.

Public Domain Pictures
www.publicdomainpictures.net/top-images.php

All pictures are royalty-free stock photos available for commercial and personal use. Some images are available for free, and others can be downloaded for a small fee.

Creative Commons (CC)
http://creativecommons.org

Creative Commons is a nonprofit organization devoted to expanding the range of creative works available for others to build upon legally and to share. The organization has released several copyright licenses, known as Creative Commons licenses, that are free of charge to the public. These licenses allow creators to communicate which rights they reserve and which rights they waive for the benefit of recipients and other creators.

STORING YOUR MATERIALS

Once you start collecting materials to use in your collage work, you'll want to devise some sort of storage system. Your storage system can be well organized, with categories for subject, color, and texture, or your materials can be randomly placed in boxes with no attention paid to cataloging the contents. Whatever works for you.

I keep my found items tucked away randomly inside plastic storage bins that I pick up at my local discount store. There is no organization to any of the contents inside the boxes because I enjoy randomly picking a box and going through it. Other artists that I know like to keep their materials neatly organized with labels so they can be easily found when needed.

Other helpful storage supplies include manila folders for storing magazine clippings or photographs. Accordion files can keep many images in one place and the partitions make for easy organizing. Flat files are great for storing larger paper items and for holding completed artwork.

If you use a lot of digital images in your work, you can store your scanned or downloaded imagery on a small external hard drive or on CDs and DVDs. I'm sure you've heard it many times before, but always back up your work. You don't want to lose all your images should your computer crash.

THE CREATIVE PROCESS

At this point, you've assembled your basic tools and materials and you have some images you'd like to use. Now what? If you need some creative guidance, you can turn to any of the Creativity Exercises beginning on page 46 and start experimenting. Or maybe you've already got an idea in mind and you're ready to play it out. In that case, go for it! If not, don't worry; the creative process is different for everyone. The good news is that you can find a way of collage making that works for you.

For me, the creative process is a physical act. I realized early on that the more I thought about creating art the less I did it. I still catch myself doing that sometimes. Ultimately, creating collage is the act of sitting down and staying open. I actually never need an idea before I start; I let the materials inform me. I encourage you to do the same: sit down and take a look at the materials in front of you. Start moving the images around. Let your materials "interact." Eventually, an idea will take root, and a story will unfold.

But first you have to look. Things start to take shape when you have a conversation with the work. It's important to know when to speak and when to listen. I usually get into trouble when I try to force an idea that I have without "listening" to what the material wants me to

Apple Basket, 2011

do. Creating a spontaneous 5-Minute collage (see page 48) is a good place to start. Sometimes the faster I make a collage, the better the results can be.

For any given collage, I start by sifting through my boxes of paper and imagery. As I look through these boxes I start to sort out little piles of paper that I like. Some are arranged by color, others by content, pattern, or whatever else I am drawn to. Next, I just start gluing things down. I'm not too worried about anything at this point. As the work progresses, I'll have to start making

more careful decisions about what to glue down next. The closer the collage is to being finished, the harder this becomes. It helps to think about how one element informs the next until the piece is finished. It's like a puzzle, and it's really satisfying when you finally figure it out. You can see how this process unwinds for me in the One Week collage on page 114. It's like getting into a rhythm and trusting the beat.

Get inspired by the images that excite you and see what happens. If you don't like something you've done, cover it up with another layer, or peel it off, or cut it out, and start again. There's no exact science to collage making. The good news is that you'll probably learn just as much by your "mistakes," and you might uncover a new way of working or a surprising solution in the process.

To inspire confidence in your own artistic process, I thought it would be helpful to include a little background on the elements and principles of design. Of course, you can skip ahead and start creating—these elements are fairly intuitive, and you may find that you subconsciously use them as you work— but they also provide a framework that can be helpful as you begin making collages, and some tools to use as you practice.

ELEMENTS OF DESIGN

Part of the creative process involves knowing the six basic elements of design and how they work in relationship to one another. These elements are the building blocks to any composition. Knowing them and putting them into practice will greatly improve your collage-making skills.

Line is an element characterized by length and direction. A line can be short or long, thin or thick. It can create a shape or show volume. It can be used to show perspective, and it can create an edge when two shapes meet. When grouped together, lines can convey texture, rhythm, and density.

Line is one of my favorite elements to use when building a composition. Showing a variety of lines moving in different directions helps lead the viewer's eye around the composition.

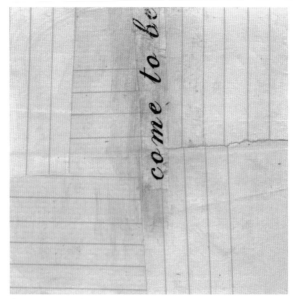

Come to Be, 2009

In this collage, I was interested in the idea of the words in the sentence creating a line. The lines on the paper also help move the viewer's eye around the piece, almost like a map.

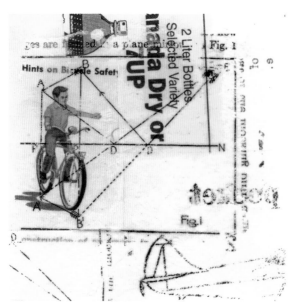

He Drank Canada Dry, 2007

Although the boy on the bicycle and the transfer of the diagram that surround him are two separate images, I like how they match. Adding diagrams is a great way to introduce line into your work.

How It Looks, 2008

Here, I used a geometric symbol to illustrate the use of line quality, and I like how the overlapping circles echo the overlapping shapes of the two men.

Shape is a self-contained area that can be geometric or organic in nature. Shape can be two-dimensional (circles, squares, triangle, or rectangles) or three-dimensional (spheres, cubes, cones, or cylinders). When a positive shape is created, it automatically creates a negative shape around it. A black silhouette of a face on a white background is a good example of this.

Texture can be visual or tactile. A texture can be smooth, rough, soft, or hard. Look for images of different kinds of textures to incorporate into your work, and consider how building up different layers of imagery and using other mediums, like paint, can add a tactile quality to your collage.

In the collages below, I used the various textures from some old books I had that were falling apart. The gauze from the bindings was especially interesting to me, and I decided to incorporate it into each piece, adding a new layer and dimensionality to the works.

Wigs, 2010

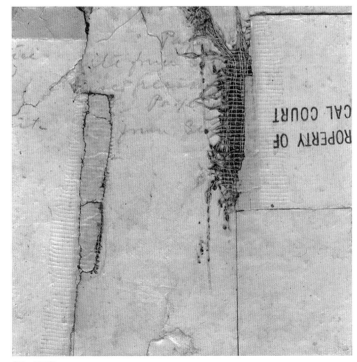

95c, 2006

The Secret, 2007

Color is one of the most exciting of the elements of design. Color can change our mood; for example, red can make us feel excited whereas blue can be calming. Color can help us define space, with warm colors like red, orange, and yellow appearing closer, and cool colors like blue, green, and purple appearing farther away.

There are three main components of color. HUE refers to pure color, one that is without tint or shade. This includes all the colors on the color wheel. VALUE is the general lightness or darkness of a color, and SATURATION is the amount of intensity, or chroma, that a color has.

COLOR HARMONY is the relationship that colors have to one another and how they can be combined to create a color palette. COMPLEMENTARY COLORS are opposite each other on the color wheel. ANALOGOUS COLORS are adjacent to one another on the color wheel. TRIADIC COLORS are equidistant, by three spaces, from one another on the color wheel. To see more examples of color in my collage work, take a look at the Color Plunge exercise on page 54. You can also try creating your own color wheel from collage scraps, like I did in the example below.

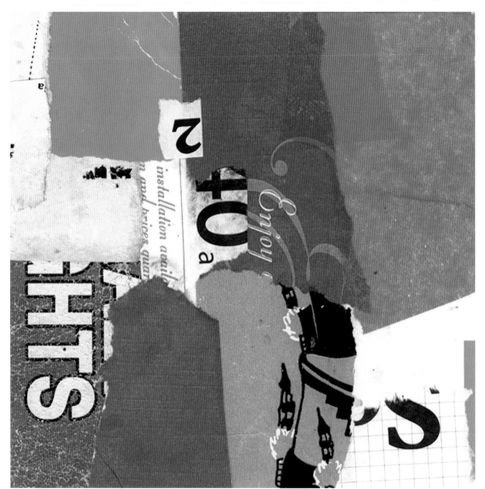

Hopscotch, 2008

In this example, I used a variety of reds to create a sense of color harmony within the piece. By using analogous colors, the collage has a warm and inviting presence to it.

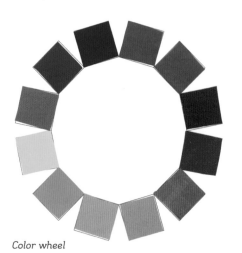

Color wheel

Value is the relationship between light and dark areas. It can also be the lightness and darkness of a color. It helps create form and gives depth and perspective. You can think of value as being on a scale of 1 to 10, with white being 1, gray falling somewhere in the middle, and black being 10. Most black-and-white photographs have a full range of values.

Space has two types, negative and positive. POSITIVE SPACE is typically space that appears to be in the front, or foreground, and NEGATIVE SPACE, or background, is the space around the positive space. Sometime a shape may be both negative and positive simultaneously. An example of this is the classic image of two profile faces that also comprise a vase.

Over Under, 2010

While making Over Under *I was concerned with giving equal attention to both the positive and the negative space of the text. This helps build a balance within the overall composition. In certain areas, white and black can be seen as being both positive and negative space.*

They May Be Giants, 2010

Notice how the image in this collage has a full range of values from white to black. If you look closely, you can see how the lines in the top right-hand portion of the collage seem to optically blend together with the white to create gray.

PRINCIPLES OF DESIGN

The principles of design are used to arrange and organize the elements of design to create a pleasing composition. When combined with the elements of design, these principles create a "recipe" for good art. Below are brief definitions of these five principles.

Balance is the visual equilibrium of objects in space. It can also be the distribution of the visual weight of colors, textures, and space. A composition can achieve balance in one of two ways: symmetrically or asymmetrically. I like to play with both of these arrangements in my work. A composition that is SYMMETRICAL will have equal weight on both sides of a centerline. When something is ASYMMETRICAL, the weight is different on each side.

Symmetry

As Is, 2007

In the example As Is, I played with another symmetrical arrangement by placing the red type close to the center. The shape on the right-hand side of the image helps balance the weight of the words on the left side to maintain equilibrium.

Becoming, 2007

In the example Becoming, I was interested in the target shape. I cut the target out of two separate images, but not right down the middle. I then placed the two halves toward the center of the paper. This created a bit of tension within the piece, but it still has equal weight, or symmetry, on both sides.

Asymmetry

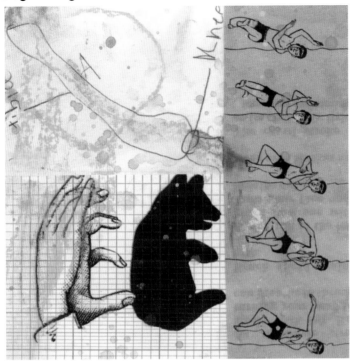

Shadowboxer, 2011

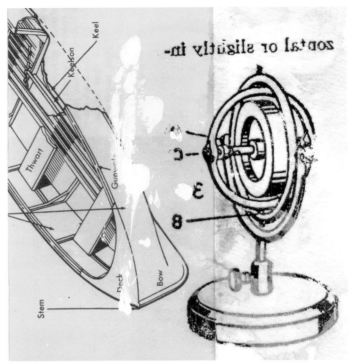

Balancing Act, 2007

The Reader, 2010

Notice how asymmetry works in the examples of Shadowboxer, Balancing Act, *and* The Reader. *Although the weight is different on each side, the rest of the collage elements work together to maintain a sense of visual unity or balance.*

Proportion refers to the various scale and size of elements within the composition and how they relate to one another, separately and as a whole. See Frankenstein on page 84 for an interesting exercise that plays with size and scale.

Modern Home, 2007

The red shape in the bottom right hand corner and the ochre shape in the top left corner appear to be in the foreground of the collage due to the size and scale of each piece, and their placement on top of the other layers. The red and white curved shape appears to be farther away because it is smaller in scale and it looks as though it is emerging from the horizon.

Emphasis helps the viewer focus on the subject of the piece. Emphasis can be created through repetition, color, and contrast. Most often, it's the central figure that shows up in the foreground. It can also be created by using the Rule of Thirds (see page 32).

Rose Letter, 2009

The emphasis in this collage is clearly the central rose; it's the focal point of the piece, with the background squares working together to bring it to the foreground.

Rhythm—just like music, art can also have rhythm. It can be seen as repeating shapes or colors. Alternating values and textures can also create rhythm within a composition.

Sure Thing, 2010

A variety of repeated shapes, including circles, squares, and flowers, creates a sense of rhythm within the piece. The variety of yellows used also creates rhythm, as it holds the collage together with a feeling of unity.

Unity is the principle that summarizes all elements and principles of design. It is a sense that all parts are working together. Pattern is one of the most fundamental elements and can create a strong sense of unity. Color can also be used to help create unity within a composition.

Oh My, 2008

In Oh My, *all the elements of design work together to create a unifying whole. Vertical and horizontal lines, the shape of the two figures in the foreground, the slight texture of the various papers, the use of color, and how the space is handled with overlapping shapes all help create unity within the collage.*

BASIC COMPOSITION

Good composition is one of the key ingredients in making a collage. Knowing where to place the elements within a design so it delivers a level of impact and balance throughout is important in creating a successful collage. Here are some basic rules that you can apply to create collage compositions that are pleasing to the eye.

The Rule of Thirds states that the artist should divide the picture into thirds, thus creating nine parts, with the main subject being placed where the lines intersect.

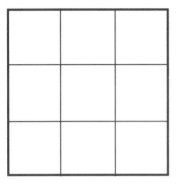

In First in Flight, *notice that the areas of interest within the composition are positioned at the intersection where the two lines meet. By placing the two figures close to these points it creates a pleasing composition. The main subject of interest can be placed on one or more of these points.*

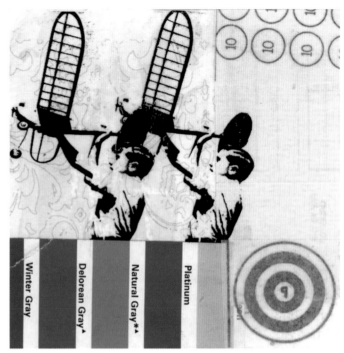

First in Flight, 2008

The Center Rule states that the main subject should be slightly off-center unless you are trying to achieve a symmetrical composition. The eye is naturally inclined to settle on a point to the right and slightly above the center of any two-dimensional image, making this an ideal place for the focal point of a collage. The centerline can also be used to divide the collage.

In Color Picker, *the girl and the grid of color samples are placed on the right-hand side of the composition and the smiley faces and geometric shapes are on the left-hand side. By placing the girl slightly off center it helps the composition become more dynamic. Think about creating pairings of two objects or a juxtaposition of two spaces divided by the centerline. You can also think about creating a design that is symmetrical or asymmetrical from the centerline (see pages 28 to 29).*

Allover Composition occurs when there isn't a clearly defined main subject or point of emphasis in the work. Instead, the overall pattern of shapes and colors creates the composition. Without a fixed focal point, all of the visual elements need to work in harmony to create a complete picture.

Although the hands in the example at right are taken from different artists' paintings, they are very similar in shape, size, and color. They are also shown on the same plane, which lends equal weight and helps create a feeling of balance.

Color Picker, 2010

History of Hands, 2010

THE COLLAGE WORKBOOK

33

LAYERING 101

Layering is an essential tool for creating a successful collage. Try to think of your collage as having three layers: background, middle ground, and foreground. The main subject of most collages is often placed in the foreground.

Think about layering the middle ground when using transfers, tracing paper, colored tissue paper, or any other transparent material. As demonstrated in the example *Crazy Weather*, the background can be a solid color, or an image, or an assortment of random patterns or textures. Notice how I build up each layer as I go along.

For me, the BACKGROUND is my favorite part of the collage to do. I start by gluing random sheets of patterned paper down first. This is where I start to choose the overall color of the collage. Next I glue down tracing paper, colored pieces of tissue paper, and other transparent material to help create the MIDDLE GROUND. This allows some of the background material to show through. As a final step, I glue down the FORE-GROUND or the subject of the collage, such as the bird in *Crazy Weather*.

Background

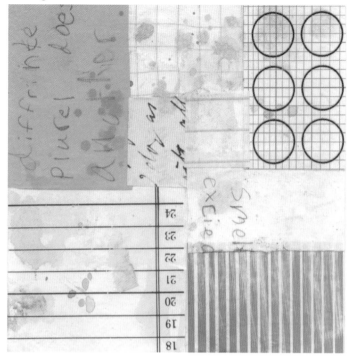

Middle ground

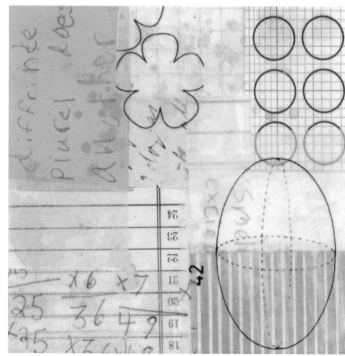

Foreground

Crazy Weather, 2011

EXPLORE

PRINTING ON TRACING PAPER

One of my favorite things to print on is tracing paper. It's great to use when you are creating multiple layers of imagery and is transparent enough to let underlying images show through. If you're concerned with permanency, there is an archival tracing paper you can buy. In this example, I created a simple collage background on a substrate for my tracing paper image to go over.

(1) Print out an image of your choice on tracing paper. There are some in the Image Library beginning on page 116 that you can try. You can always print multiple images on one sheet and cut them out for individual use later. Note that you may have to place a clear piece of transparent tape on the bottom half of the sheet to get it to feed through the rollers of your printer. After printing the sheet, cut out your image.

(2) Spray your image with two light coats of UV protectant. Allow the first coat to dry thoroughly before applying the second coat. This will keep the ink from running when you apply the matte medium. After the protectant is dry, cut around your image.

(3) Use a soft sable brush to apply a thin coat of acrylic matte medium to the back side of the image. Be very careful when doing this, because the paper will begin to curl.

(4) Position your image where you want it to be in your collage.

(5) Use a brayer or the palm of your hand to flatten the tracing paper and smooth out any creases. If you have any excess overlap from your image, trim accordingly. I usually follow up by applying another coat of protectant and then a coat of acrylic gloss or matte medium to seal the collage.

TOOLS + MATERIALS

Tracing or velum paper
Ink-jet printer
Transparent tape (if needed)
Clear matte UV protectant spray
Soft sable watercolor brush
Acrylic matte medium
Scissors
Substrate or support
Hard rubber brayer

①

②

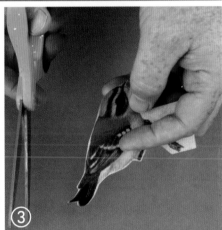

③

④

⑤

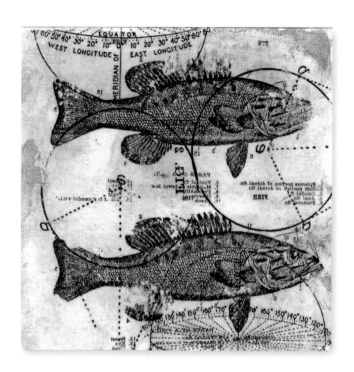

LASER TRANSFERS USING TRACING PAPER

This is one of my favorite techniques for creating a transfer. A good laser printer can be acquired inexpensively, and the toner cartridges that are included with the printer can produce thousands of images before needing to be replaced.

(1) Print out an image of your choice on tracing paper. There are some in the Image Library beginning on page 116 that you can try. You can always print multiple images on one sheet and cut them out for individual use later. Note that you may have to place a clear piece of transparent tape on the bottom half of the sheet to get it to feed through the rollers of your printer. After printing the sheet, cut out your image, leaving at least a 1-inch (2.5 cm) border around it.

(2) Coat the toner side of the image with acrylic matte medium using a soft sable brush. Be generous with the medium, and make sure the image is evenly coated.

(3) Place the tracing paper, image side down, onto your substrate. Note: If the surface of the substrate is hard and smooth, the toner will transfer better. Avoid using substrates that are soft and absorbent.

(4) Use the brayer to roll the tracing paper onto the collage. Make sure it is flat and even.

(5) After about 20 to 30 seconds, peel back a small corner of the tracing paper; you don't want to let the tracing paper adhere to the substrate. Slowly lift the tracing paper away from the substrate to see if the toner is lifting, but do not pull it completely away because you may need to apply more medium if the image is not transferring.

(6) As you can see, the transfer is a mirror image of the original; if you're transferring words or numbers, they'll print backwards, like in this example.

TOOLS + MATERIALS

Laser printer

Tracing paper
(no need to use archival)

Transparent tape (if needed)

Scissors

Acrylic matte medium

Soft sable watercolor brush

Substrate or support

Hard rubber brayer

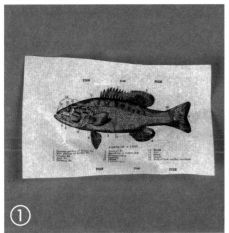

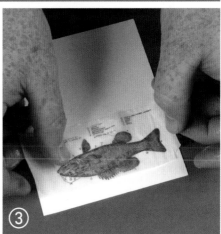

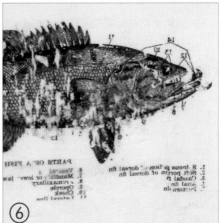

Carnivore, 2010

INK TRANSFERS USING TRANSPARENCY FILM

Clear transparency film can be found in most office supply stores or online. Look for the kind that is used with ink-jet printers.

① Choose an image in either black and white or color that you'd like to transfer. (Turn to the Image Library on page 116 for some options.) Make sure the image is at least 150 dpi. Load the clear transparency film into your printer with the rough side facing up. Print your image and cut it out.

② Coat the Bristol board with a generous and even layer of acrylic gloss medium using a foam brush.

③ Place the transparency, ink side down, onto the Bristol board.

④ Apply pressure to the back of the transparency using a bone folder or the back of a spoon. Wait a few seconds and then carefully peel back part of the transparency to see if the image lifted onto the board. Timing is key here: the gloss medium should not be too wet or too dry. If the medium is still too wet, the ink will run, and if it is too dry, the transparency will stick to the board. Experiment using small cut pieces of transparency until you get the hang of it.

⑤ The final result will be a little different each time. Keep practicing until you get a feel for what works best.

TOOLS + MATERIALS

Digital imagery (scanned or found on the Internet)

Clear transparency film

Ink-jet printer with pigmented ink

Scissors

Bristol board

Acrylic gloss medium

Foam brush

Bone folder or spoon

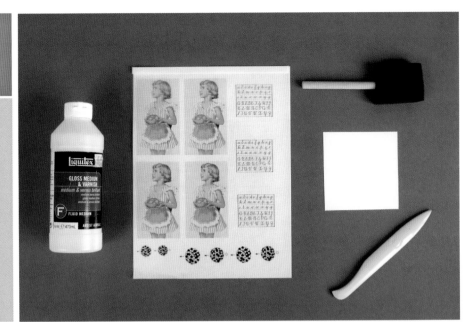

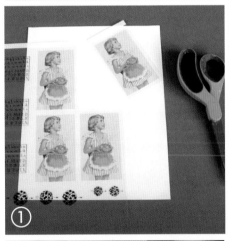

①

②

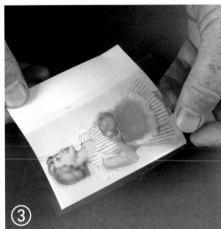

③

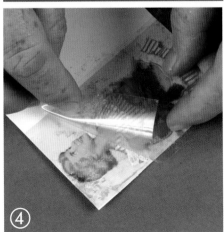

④

⑤

MATTING YOUR WORK

Matting and framing your artwork will protect it from the elements, such as harmful UV light, dust, and humidity, and will increase the life span of your collage. When choosing the color of your mat, I find it best to stay with neutral colors so that your work remains the focal point of the piece. I typically use various shades of white. In my experience, white has a tendency to both brighten and complement the artwork, and it looks great in any frame.

CUTTING MAT BOARD

You'll need the following supplies to cut your own mats.

Mat board is the board that protects your artwork from touching the glass. It is available in precut sheets and in 32 x 40-inch (81.3 x 101.6 cm) sheets. It is also available in both 2-ply (about the thickness of Bristol board) and 4-ply (1⁄16 inch [1.5 mm]). I recommend choosing the thicker 4-ply mat board, and one that is archival, if available.

Foam board, also known as backing board, is what your artwork rests on. It is available in various sizes and thicknesses and comes in both black and white. Choose a foam board that is archival, if possible.

Mat cutters come in a variety of sizes and vary in price. If you plan on cutting a lot of mats for your work, it's worth investing in one that can cut larger sizes and has guide marks for more accurate cutting. Be sure to stock up on plenty of blades. Depending on the size of your mats, you will be able to cut between ten and twenty mats per blade.

Archival mounting tape can be found at most art supply stores. It looks like an ordinary roll of masking tape, but it can be peeled off and repositioned without tearing the back side of the artwork. The paper and the glue on the tape are both archival and will not yellow over time.

NOTE: In this example, I demonstrate how to float a 4 x 4-inch (10.2 x 10.2 cm) collage inside a 1¾-inch (4.4 cm) bordered mat, with measurements given to reflect this size. For your own artwork, adjust the measurements accordingly.

TOOLS + MATERIALS

Ruler

T square

Utility knife

Mat board (shown already cut)

Foam board

Pencil

Mat cutter

Emery board

Bone folder

Archival mounting tape

Gum eraser

Collage

① Start by measuring your artwork. It is a good idea to leave at least a 1¾-inch (4.4 cm) border on smaller work and a 3¾-inch (9.5 cm) border on larger works, allowing ¼ inch (6 mm) for the image to float inside the mat.

② Using a T square and a utility knife, measure and cut an 8 x 8-inch (20.3 x 20.3 cm) square of mat board and foam board.

③ Mark a 1¾-inch (4.4 cm) border around each side of the mat board using a pencil on the back side of the mat.

④ Cut out the square using a mat cutter. Pay special attention when you get close to the corners.

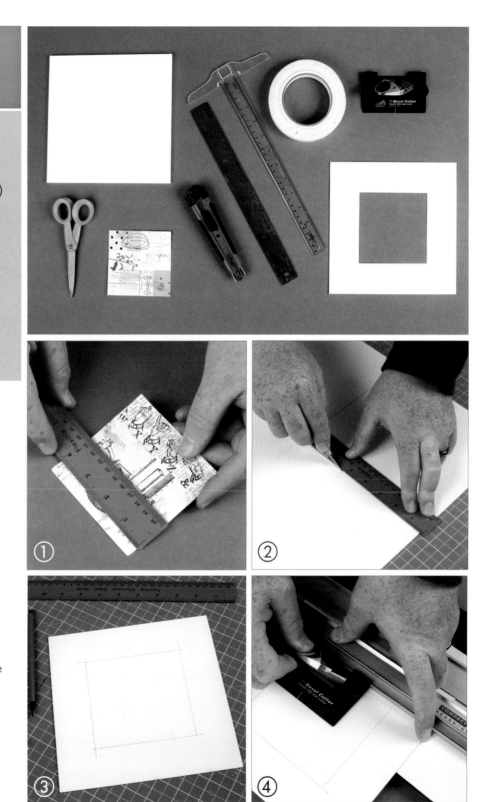

⑤ When the cut is complete, examine the corners for a clean edge. You can always use an emery board and bone folder if you need to clean up an edge.

⑥ Apply a 7-inch (17.8 cm) strip of archival mounting tape along the inside top of the mat board and mount it on the foam board.

⑦ Erase any pencil marks and dust off the crumbs.

⑧ Apply pieces of folded archival tape to the back side of the collage and position it in the mat opening on the front.

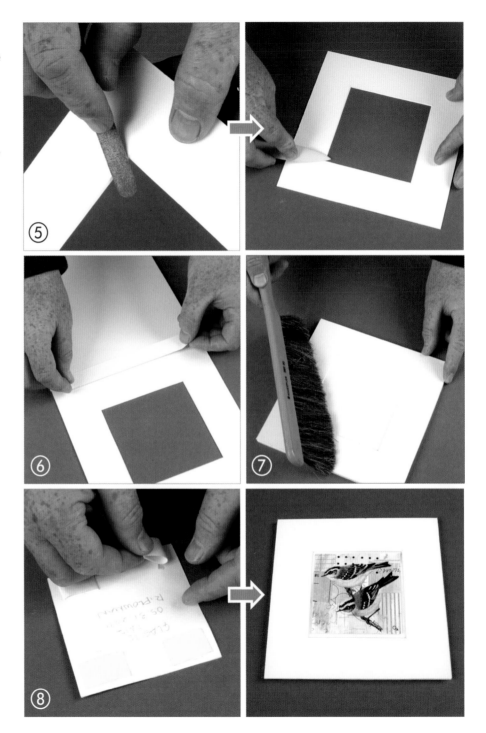

BUILDING A HOME PRESS

Depending on the type and size of support you use, you may find that your collage begins to bow and curl as you glue down the layers. One way to keep your finished piece perfectly flat is to use a simple press. I built one of these years ago, and have been using one ever since. Since I like to float my collages inside a mat (see page 42) it's important that the artwork stays flat and does not curl up at the corners and off the backing board. With some simple, inexpensive supplies, and easy assembly, this press does the trick.

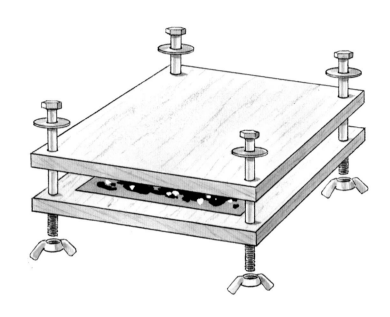

MATERIALS

Two wood squares cut to 12 x 12 inches (30.5 x 30.5 cm) each

Four ¼-inch (6 mm) hex head bolts, each 5-inches (12.7 cm) long

Eight ¼-inch washers

Four ¼-inch wing nuts

① If you don't have the equipment to cut wood at home, you can buy what you need at a home center and have them cut the wood for you. I like to use pine shelving for my presses.

② Drill ¼-inch (6 mm) holes at least 1-inch (2.5 cm) in on all corners of each pine board. Take care to ensure the holes line up on both boards.

③ Stack both boards. Slip a washer on each hex head bolt and insert the bolts through the holes of the boards.

④ Slip a washer and wing nut on the end of each hex head bolts. To insert your artwork, loosen the wing nuts and make space between the boards. To press, tighten the wing nuts and leave your collage to dry and flatten overnight.

Tip: *To protect your artwork in the press, use pieces of heavy cardboard or mat board to sandwich your artwork on either side.*

Tip: *If you want to press a collage after it's already dried, you can spray a light mist of water on the back side of the collage and then put it in the press overnight.*

50 CREATIVITY EXERCISES

Gather your scraps, glue, and scissors and jump right in! You can follow these prompts in the order they appear, and build up your skills playing with color, layering, and transfer techniques, or you can begin wherever you like. For added inspiration, turn to the Image Library on page 116 and see what images spark your creativity. If you feel stuck, try another exercise. If you stay open and spontaneous in your exploration, your collage will take on a life of its own.

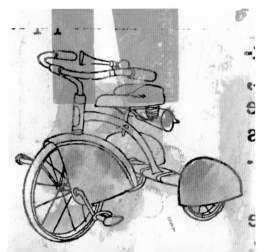

ROLD

DIAMOND-BACK
RATTLESNAKE

TIMBER, RATTLESNAKE

PRAIRIE
RATTLESNAKE

SIDEWINDER
OR HORNED
RATTLE
SNAKE

WATER

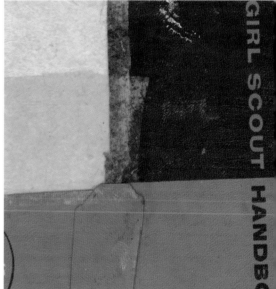

GIRL SCOUT HANDBO

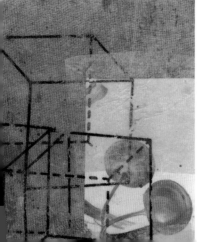

/50

FIVE 5-MINUTE COLLAGES

Make five, 5-minute collages on 3 x 5-inch (7.6 x 12.7 cm) heavy watercolor paper. You'll find this exercise really freeing—without time to overthink what you're doing, the results will be intuitive and interesting.

To begin, simply go through some magazines and cut out the pictures and pieces of imagery that catch your eye. If you have some images preprinted on tracing paper (page 36), put these in the mix, too. When you think you have enough, set a timer for 5 minutes and get to work!

The trick is to keep your hands moving—picking out images, playing with arranging them, and then gluing them down. When the timer goes off, pull out more images and move on to the next collage. Twenty-five minutes later you'll be surprised at what you just created.

Untitled, 2011

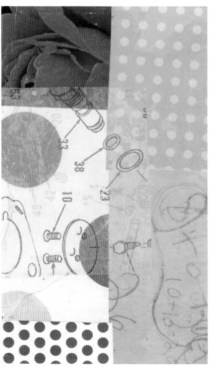

Untitled, 2011

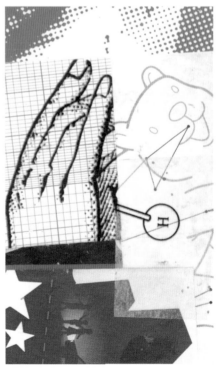

Untitled, 2011

rd problems....

ection 5.7 that, at a
ture, the velocity of a
s mass are inversely

Untitled, 2011

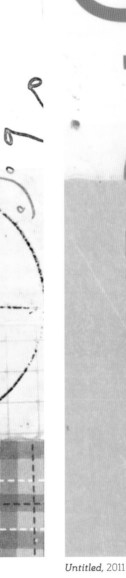

H_2Se

H_2S

AsH_3

HCl

HB

GeH

SiH_4

Untitled, 2011

2 WHITE OUT

Make a collage using various shades of white only. Consider using materials such as old book pages, envelopes, tissue paper, and tracing paper. This is a great exercise to begin playing with different shapes and subtle shifts in color.

DYO, 2007

I, Me, Mine, 2007

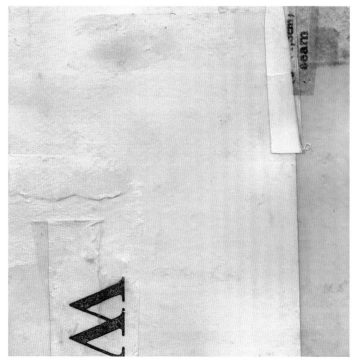

Falling, 2006

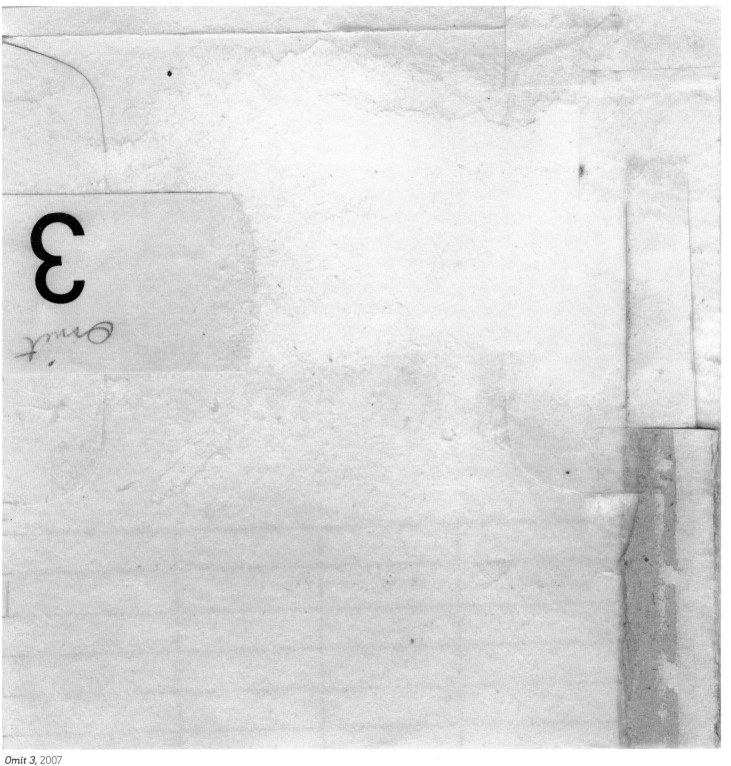

Omit 3, 2007

BLACK & WHITE

Try creating a collage using only black and white imagery. Pay attention to the differences in value from white to black (see page 27 for a refresher), and play with ways to balance the light and dark elements of your composition.

Nosecone, 2007

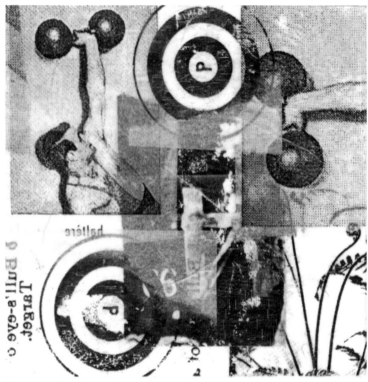

Target, 2007

COLOR CHARGE

Experiment with applying color to a collage that's primarily black and white. A few subtle strokes and bright marks can make a subdued collage really pop. In *Breath,* I used watercolor crayon to add another layer to the collage; they work great for both opaque and transparent color (see page 17).

Breath, 2008

COLOR PLUNGE

Choose a color and make a monochromatic collage using various shades of that color only (or mostly). Why stop there? Try making a collage for every color in the rainbow. This is a great exercise to explore the power of color and how you can integrate it into your work. For more information on color and the color wheel, turn to page 26.

Sentimental Pick, 2010

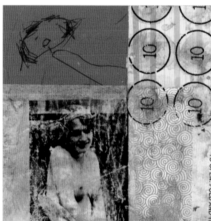

Do-si-do, 2008

Dada Da, 2008

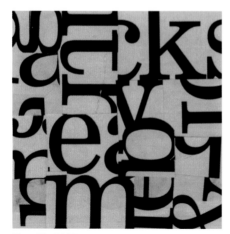

Toss-Up, 2009

Missing Link, 2007

Deep Edge, 2007

Yellow Is Yellow, 2008

Of It All, 2008

How To, 2009

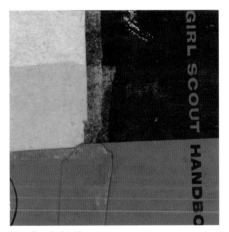

Handbook, 2007

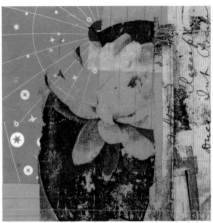

The Lotus, 2008

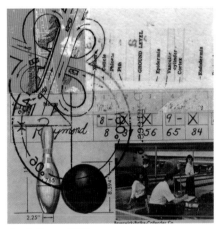

Ray's Score, 2007

Moonpie, 2008

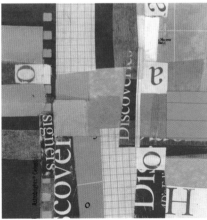

In Pictures, 2009

Sister, 2006

IMAGE PAIRINGS

Cut an image in half and pair each half with other images and decorative elements to create two distinctly different collages. As you work, notice how something as simple as an unexpected pairing can create a new visual relationship and a unified "story" between subjects.

Knockout, 2010

Next Big Thing, 2010

THE COLLAGE WORKBOOK

STRIPS

Pick two or three different images and cut them into thin strips of approximately the same size. Assemble a collage alternating the image strips to create an entirely new image. For this piece, I worked with a general theme of flowers, but you can also play with mixing dramatically different images.

Push and Pull, 2006

8

REASSEMBLE

Take an image and cut it up into squares of the same size. Then, reassemble the squares into a new collage, experimenting with turning the pieces at different angles.

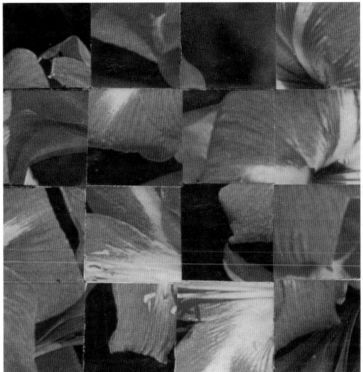

Reassemble the Flower, 2011

SQUARES & RECTANGLES

Instead of cutting strips like the exercise on page 58, cut squares or rectangles from two or more images and try mixing and matching them to create a new point of view. It's like creating a two-dimensional patchwork quilt.

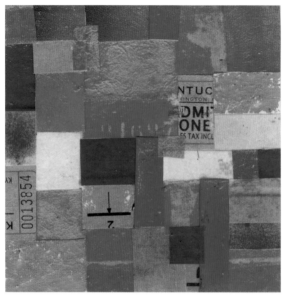

36 Blues, 2006

29 Views, 2006

Mixed Flowers, 2006

21 Greens, 2006

Turnaround, 2006

DÉCOLLAGE

Create a collage by layering pieces of paper with interesting colors and images on top of one another. Before the glue sets, begin tearing away the top layers of paper to reveal the imagery underneath. If you're using imagery from a magazine or newspaper, this will often create a transfer effect, revealing the underside of the image.

Here you can see the fifth layer on the front. I slowly start to peel away pieces of each layer to reveal the layers beneath.

Once I'm happy with the deconstructed composition, I finish the collage with a coat of protective varnish.

Happy Blues, 2011

The Follow Through, 2011

NUMBERS

Make a collage that focuses on numbers, either spelled out or in numeric form. You can go through a magazine to source numbers, or you can print out your own in fonts that you like. Consider even using scrap calculations or a lucky number if you have one.

Ten, 2010

Her Thoughts, 2009

Tulsa Time, 2009

Your Lucky 7, 2008

TYPOGRAPHY

12

Building off of the Numbers exercise, construct a collage using found type from magazines or newspapers. Take it a step further and cut out pieces of the words, or letters, and overlap them in various directions to create a new kind of visual language.

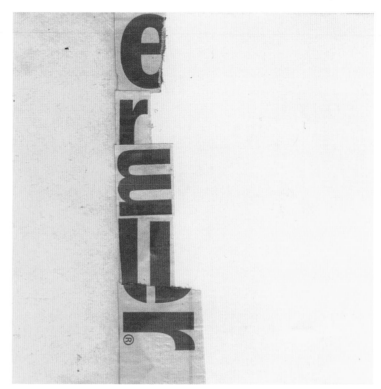

Trouble with Time, 2007

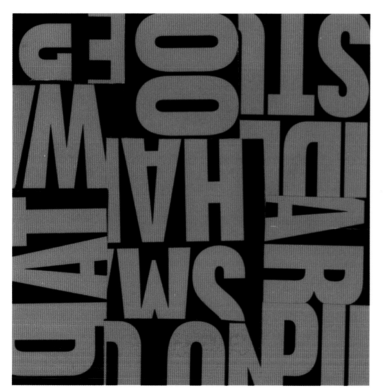

Shazam, 2010

Stop Making Sense, 2007

...yme or Reason, 2010

Word Up, 2009

...s-Up, 2009

Inside Out, 2008

SECRET MESSAGE

This is a riff on the Typography exercise. Pick a name, word, phrase, or song title, and either print it out in a pleasing font or search for the letters of your word or words in magazines. Using only these letters (or parts of them), create an abstract collage. The casual onlooker may not realize the "message" contained in each artwork, but your title can offer a clue.

Knockout, 2010

For e. e. cummings, 2007

Busy Day, 2010

STAMPS

Using stamps in your collage can create an additional layer of intrigue. These examples show office materials that were stamped, but you can also try playing with a host of rubber stamp imagery or even carve your own linoleum stamp.

Crossword, 2008

Discard, 2007

15

OLD BOOKS

Give an old book a second life by turning parts of it into a collage. Old hardcover books can be used both as substrates and as design elements—especially if they have interesting cover designs or fabric that piques your interest.

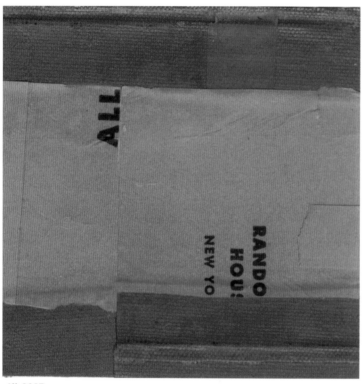

All, 2007

Modern Physics, 2007

16 UPSIDE DOWN

As with the Image Pairings exercise (page 56), try using two different images to create a single collage, but, as a twist, flip one of the images for a more dynamic effect. You'll want to pay special attention to where the images "connect" in order to create a balanced composition.

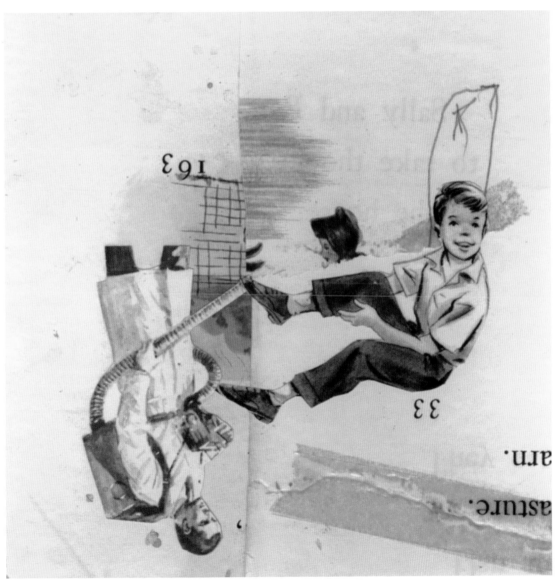

Floater, 2010

FINGER PAINT

Unleash your inner kindergartner and add splashes of color to a collage using your fingers and some acrylic paint. The effect can be surprisingly sophisticated. Look for an opening in your collage and give it a try. You can always practice on a scrap piece of paper first, if you want. If you aren't happy with it, and you act quickly, you can always wipe it off.

Forever Again, 2009

This Time Around, 2006

TISSUE PAPER

Experiment with adding pieces of colored tissue paper to a collage to create sheer layers that enhance and slightly mask the images that lie beneath.

All about F89, 2006

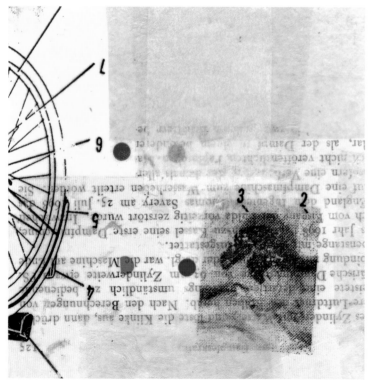

Mr. Universe, 2006

Seeing Her, 2007

What Once Was, 2010

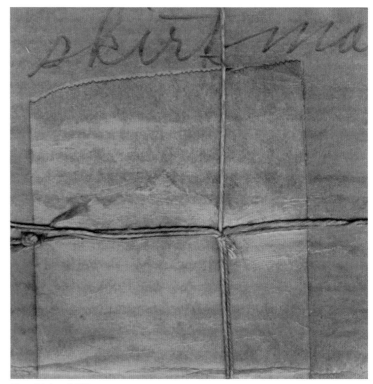

Skirt Maker, 2008

Part One, 2006

19

CARDBOARD

Use cardboard in your collage as a background support or even as an added layer. Thick cardboard can achieve an interesting effect, and if it's corrugated, you can try using it like a stamp.

MAPS

Dig out some maps and use pieces of them in your collage. They might be left over from a vacation, show your home state, or be places you've always wanted to go. In this same vein, you could also play with subway maps or bus routes in your work.

Frontiersman, 2010

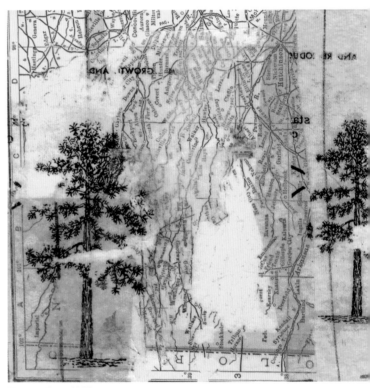

Kansas Tree, 2006

TREASURE HUNT

Take a walk and keep your eyes open for found scraps, handwritten lists, notes, or other elements you can use in your collages. I found this piece of paper on the ground during a recent walk to my studio and was drawn to the flower pattern and color printer bar. Keep your eyes open—you never know what you'll find, and it could be the perfect piece to activate your next collage.

The Letter, 2011

STORYBOOK

Go through a children's story-book for imagery you'd like to use. If the book is precious to you, you can always scan and print the pages if you don't want to use the originals. If you stumble upon some scribbles from long ago, consider adding even more to your collage. It's all part of the story.

Me, Me, Me, 2010

Gravy Train, 2010

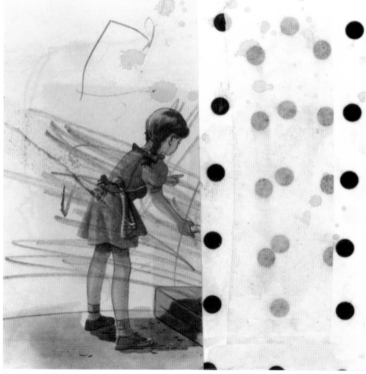

Soapbox, 2010

Hula Hoop, 2010

HANDS

Hands can be wonderfully expressive. Look for pictures of hands in different poses and create a collage using hands as the focal element. This can create a new, nonverbal meaning depending on the kind of gestures you choose. If you like, you can try creating a collage using only pictures of hands, like I did in *History of Hands* (page 33).

The Flower, 2009

Shadow Play, 2010

The Conversationalist, 2010

Playhouse, 2011

24

HOME

Pick images, colors, and types of paper to accurately convey what the term "home" means to you. This can be literal or abstract. You can even take it a step further and recreate your neighborhood using different images of houses and people.

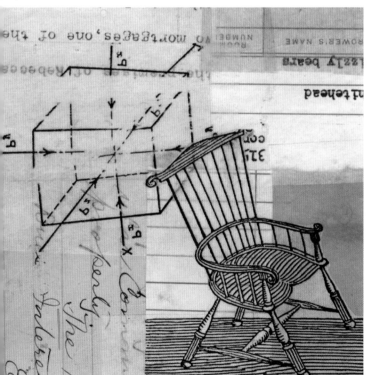

Art of Sitting, 2008

Lifelike, 2010

THE COLLAGE WORKBOOK

81

SEEING DOUBLE

Experiment with transferring and layering the same image in a collage more than once. Notice how repetition can create a unique pattern when you play around with the possibilities. You can try overlapping your images to create a kind of halo or double-vision effect, you can intentionally leave some space to emphasize the repetition, or you can play with flipping an image to create a mirror effect.

Worlds Apart, 2008

Missile, 2006

Double, 2007

zzle, 2007

Blue Speckled Hen, 2008

nnel Cakes, 2006

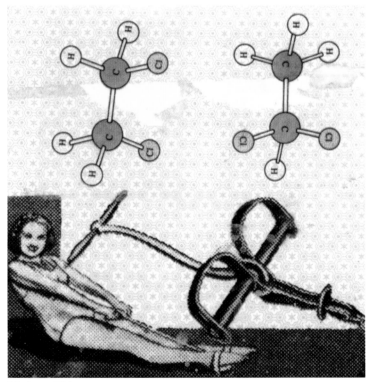

Workout, 2010

FRANKENSTEIN

Collect different images of people and create an entirely new character using different parts of the figures. You can really play with size and scale for this one.

Frankenstein, 2011

RECYCLE

Create a collage out of things you find in your recycling bin. Those junk mailers, bills, catalogs, coupons, and food packaging will take on an entirely new meaning when you view them as visual elements.

Any Given Sunday, 2008

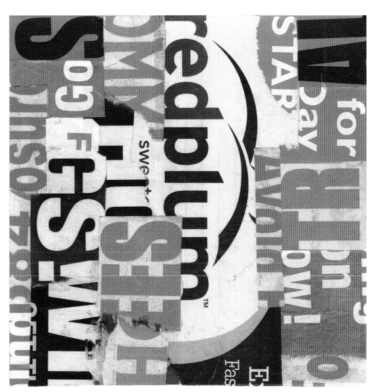

Red Plum Tree, 2008

FLORA

Make a collage using pictures of flowers. You can use images from old home and garden magazines, photos of your own flowerbed, or even seed packet imagery. This is a great exercise to play with colors found in nature.

Lovestruck, 2009

Roses, 2011

For You, 2008

Two Flowers, 2001

Dancer, 2009

Nature's Painting, 2008

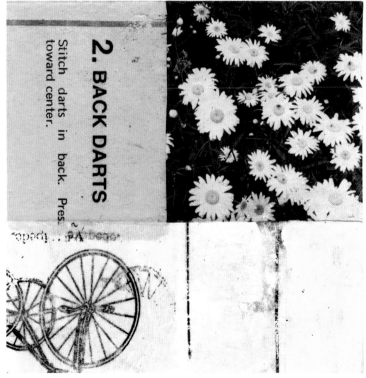

Daisies, 2006

BIRD WATCH

Birds show up a lot in my collage work. To me, birds represent freedom and spirituality. I see them as a link between the heavens and the earth, and as a symbol of rebirth and resurrection. In East Indian mythology, every bird in the world represents a departed soul, and in Christian art, birds often appear as saved souls.

Nest Builder, 2011

Diamond Rings, 2008

Fancy Thing, 2010

Cluck Clucker, 2008

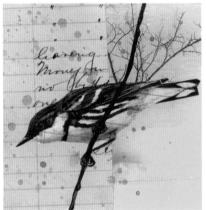

Foot Pedals, 2010

Treetop Flyer, 2010

First Class, 2008

She Tried, 2010

DREAM

I based this collage on a dream I had where a friend and I were lost in Belgium. The grid format I used made me think of a map of the city. Try translating one of your dreams into a collage and see what you discover.

Had a Dream of Belgium, 2008

MANIFEST

Create a collage around something you desire. It can be something abstract or specific.

For *Hobo*, I was inspired after reading a story about retired couples selling their homes and buying small campers to tour the United States. In *Traveler*, I focused on a desire to travel to different places all over the world.

Hobo, 2009

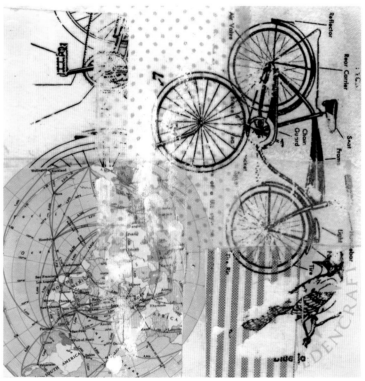

Traveler, 2006

SCAN ONLY

Create four 6 x 6-inch (15.2 x 15.2 cm) collages by placing images at random on your scanner. Print the scans out and glue them onto a sheet of heavy cardstock. This is a great lesson in keeping your collages loose and staying open to the element of surprise.

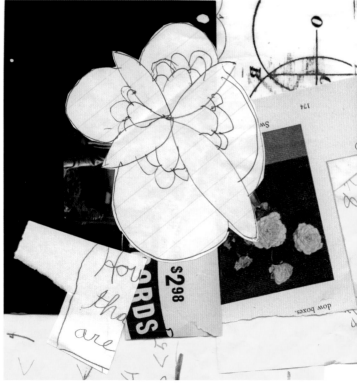

CHARLOTTE ARMSTRONG
(Pat. 455)
is a very large-flowered,
sturdy Hybrid Tea

Yellow-billed

FINGERPRINT

Dab your thumb in an inkpad and stamp your fingerprint on a piece of paper. Then, scan your fingerprint at the highest resolution possible. Print it out and use it as a pattern, texture, background element, or transfer in your collage.

For this exercise, I scanned my fingerprint at 3600 dpi and changed the color using image-editing software. For fun, I cut the image into squares and put it together in the same way as the Reassemble exercise on page 59.

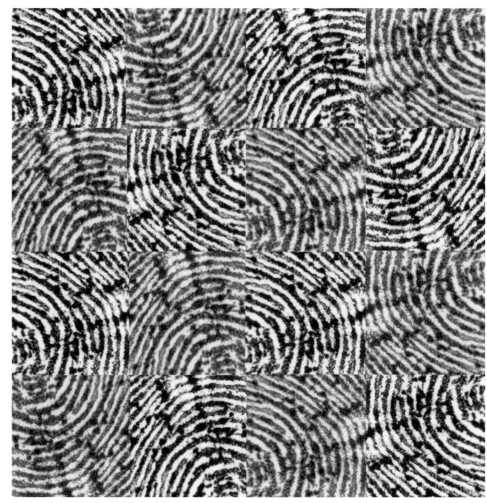

Fingerprint Typography, 2011

Mr. Fix It, 2006

HOROSCOPE

Create a collage based on a horoscope or fortune cookie. Your piece can be as literal or as cryptic as the message you're illustrating.

Horoscope: Now is the time to fix things around the house.

Smiling Device, 2007

Fortune: Smiling will make you look and feel younger.

FAVORITE PASTIME

Do you have a favorite pastime? I've always been a fan of baseball, especially the Cincinnati Reds, and am really interested in the golden age of the sport during the 1920s. Most players didn't make a lot of money during that time, but played for the love of the sport. These collages are my homage to these players, and to their passion for the game.

Maybe you played a sport in school or have always cheered for a certain team. Or maybe you have a favorite hobby. Whatever it is, gather photos and images that reflect your interest and make a collage that focuses on that theme. You can look for historic photos of your idols, or even dig through your old yearbooks and make a collage of your glory days.

Extension, 2008

Next Big Thing, 2010

AD SPACE

Manipulate a print ad to create a new message. Peruse magazines or newspapers or use one of the vintage scans in the Image Library (page 116).

Go Go, 2010

epwalker, 2001

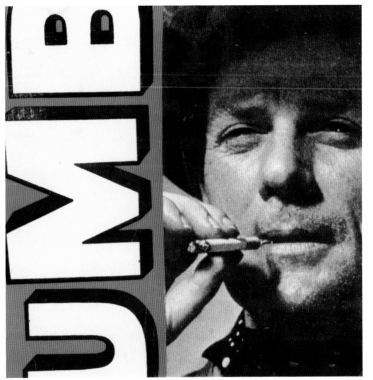

Bogart, 2010

POWER LINES

I'm fascinated with power lines on a formal level because of the lines they create in space. It's as if someone has taken a marker and drawn in the sky. For this exercise, find or take pictures of power lines and use them as a design element in your collage.

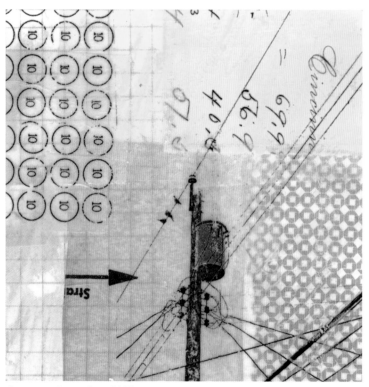

Cincinnati Power Line, 2008

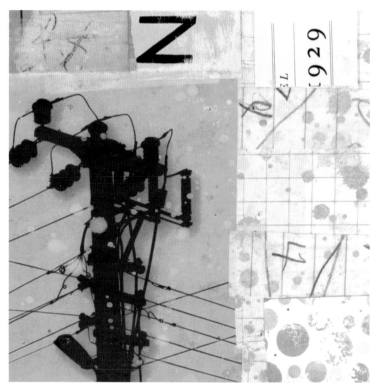

Storm, 2010

Lines, 2008

COMICS

Using an old comic book (preferably not *Superman #1*), cut out some panels and images and create an abstract arrangement to tell a new story.

Kapow, 2011

Quit Pulling My Leg, 2010

TRANSPORTATION

Incorporate wheels or various modes of transport into your collage. Personally, I'm fascinated with the design of bicycles, especially the wheels. There's something pleasing about the symmetry and the alignment of the spokes, and circles have a way of pulling a composition together. Living in Madison, Wisconsin, I bike most everywhere around the city. I guess you could say bicycles have become a symbol of my everyday life. What's yours?

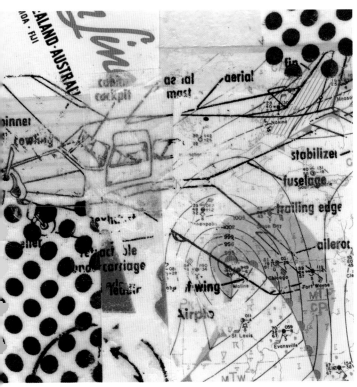

Stream, 2006

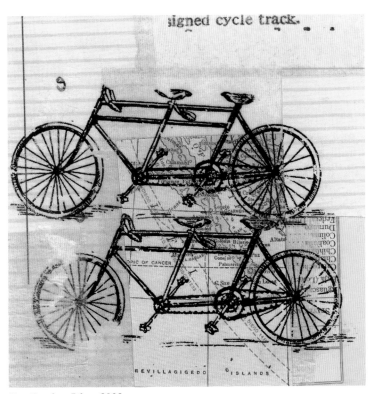

Two Tandem Bikes, 2006

HANDWRITING

Use pieces of found handwriting to enhance or take center stage in a collage. Dig through old letters, shop for vintage postcards, or use some of your own old notes or shopping lists. To get started right away, use one of the found notes in the Image Library (page 116).

Shout Out, 2010

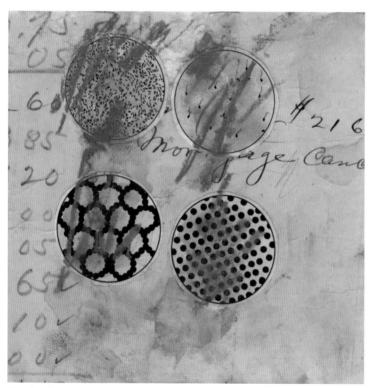

Two for the Money, 2008

Winter Discontent, 2002

SEWING PATTERN

Make a collage using one or more old sewing patterns. Experiment with using the thin pattern paper as an element or even as a transfer. You can also consider using the illustrated figures found on pattern envelopes.

Half Patterns, 2007

Polka, 2006

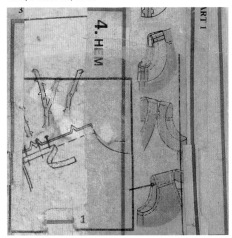

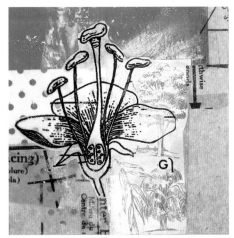

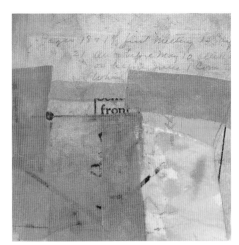

Art, 2006

Flower Parts with G, 2006

First Meeting, 2006

42 PAST, PRESENT, FUTURE

Make a collage that reflects your view of the past, present, and future.

Past

The Goodbye, 2009

Present

Enjoy Color, 2010

Future

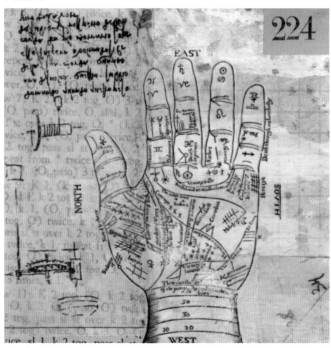

Southern Code, 2009

DIAGRAMS

Create a simple collage in one color scheme and play with superimposing a diagram transfer over it. I frequently use diagrams as design elements in my work, and enjoy the juxtaposition of man-made shapes with those found in nature. You can find diagram images in dictionaries, in textbooks, and online, or you can use some of the ones I've provided in the Image Library (page 116).

Pilot, 2010

d Jar, 2007

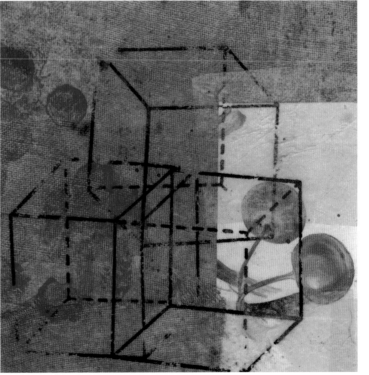

Square Dance, 2007

REPURPOSED ARTWORK

Cut up older artwork that you're not happy with and use that to make a collage. It could be an old drawing, a watercolor painting, or even a collage. In these examples, I made some fluid paint marks on paper and later reassembled them into something new and more dynamic.

Before

After

In Translation, 2011

SELF-PORTRAIT

Make a collage that's a self-portrait. You can work from photos or use imagery you feel reflects who you are. For my self-portrait, I used a little stick figure that I found drawn in the back of an old math textbook. I identify with the expression on the figure's face because I've always preferred drawing over math, too!

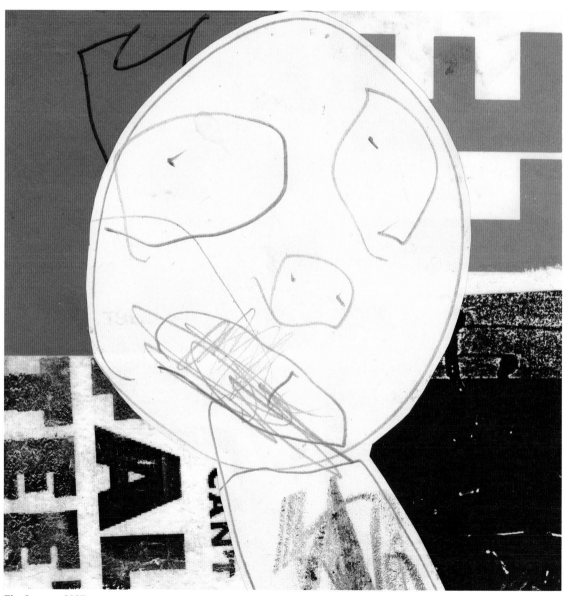

The Scream, 2007

46

CHILD'S PLAY

Collaborate with a child on a collage. You can transfer images of his or her original drawings, doodles, or markings, or you can build a collage together, alternating piece by piece and seeing what you come up with.

Magic Wand, 2010

Four Boats, 2007

Birds are Scary, 2008

THE COLLAGE WORKBOOK

47

PHOTO COLLAGE

Copy or scan a photograph that's meaningful to you to use as an element or a transfer. Old black-and-white photos are always interesting to play with, and if you have the software, you can manipulate a photo in any number of ways.

Day for Night, 2010

Spelling Lesson, 2006

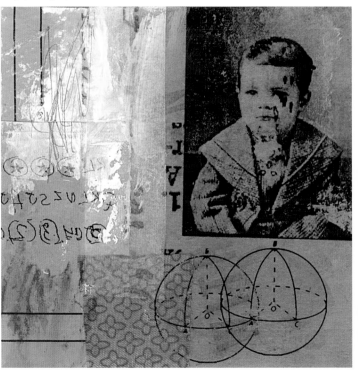

Once Upon a Time, 2008

The Town, 2009

FOUR SEASONS

Create four collages, one for each season. Consider the colors and textures that resonate for you within each of those seasons as you create each piece.

Wonder of Spring, 2008

Lost Summer, 2007

Fall Leaves, 2010

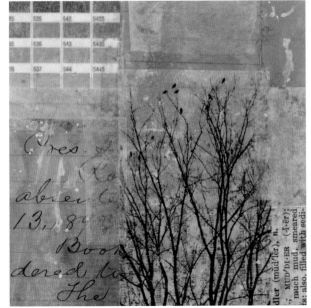

Naked Winter, 2008

49

A PICTURE ON EVERY PAGE

Make a collage using something you find on each page of an old magazine. It can be bits of text or found imagery, but the challenge is to put it all together in one unified collage.

Hit Parade, 2011

ONE WEEK

Make a collage over the course of one week by adding only one item per day. If you're ever feeling overwhelmed with creating a collage in one sitting, this is a good method to try. You only have to commit to one piece of the puzzle a day!

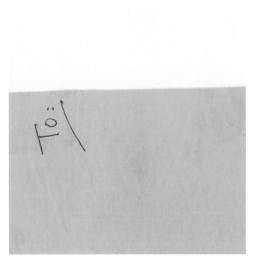
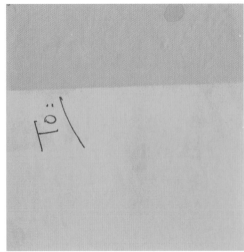

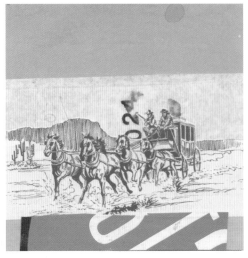

Technicolor, 2011

IMAGE LIBRARY

Collecting imagery is one of the most exciting things about collage. Feel free to use the images provided here to get you started, but don't limit yourself to just these. Copyright-free imagery can be found everywhere, including the Internet (see page 21), and books that feature clip art. You can also go to www.acollageaday.com for links to download these and other copyright-free images to use in your work.

Scanning the images in the Image Library will allow you to print them on the paper of your choice, including tracing paper and transparency film to create transfers (see pages 36 to 41). Remember that your transfer will be a mirror image of the original, which means that words will print backwards, unless they're already reversed. That's why some of the accompanying text in the Image Library is backwards; it's intentional! Scanning the images will also allow you to re-size them to use in whatever format you wish. If you want the images to be larger, try scanning them at 600 dpi or higher.

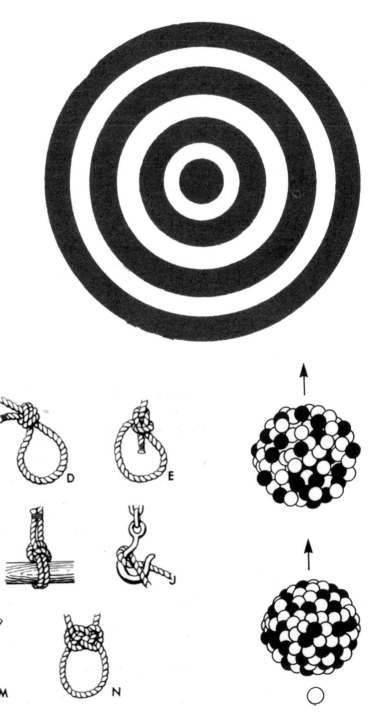

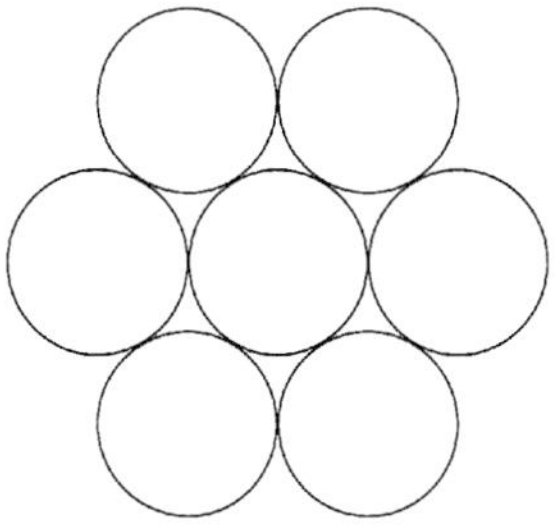

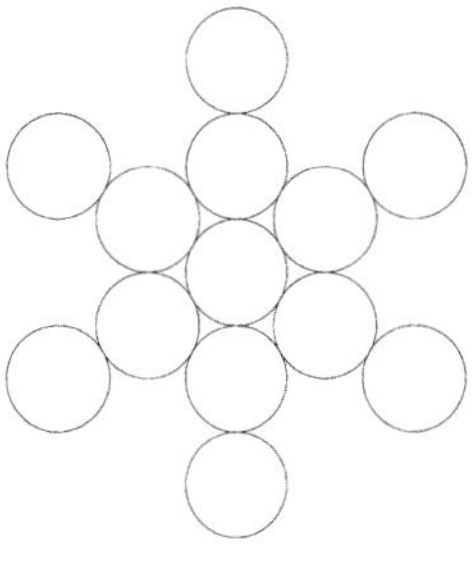

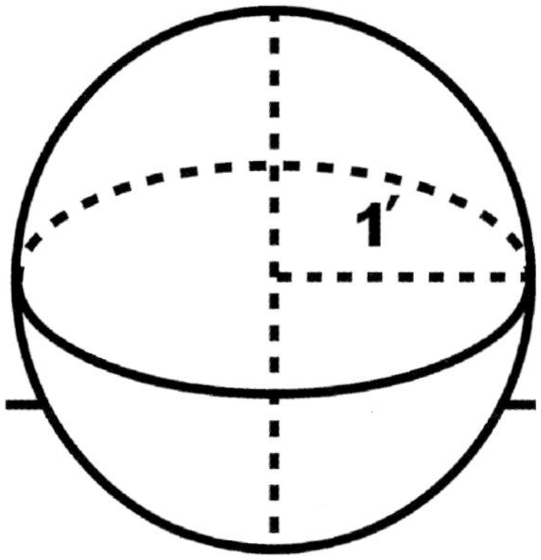

Li
(1.52)

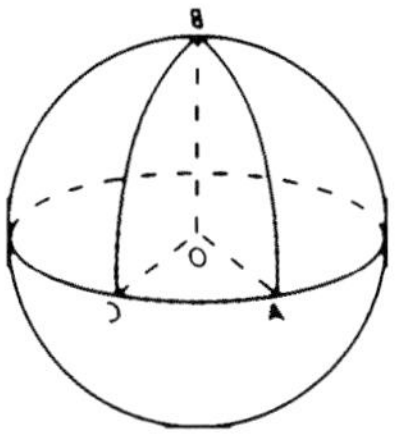

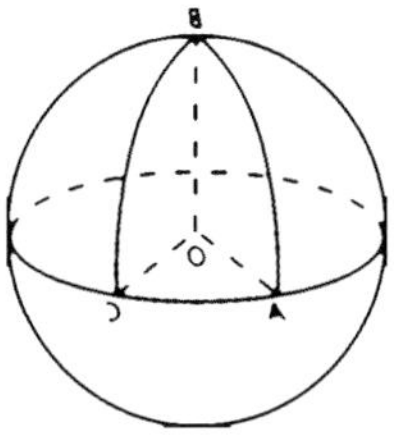

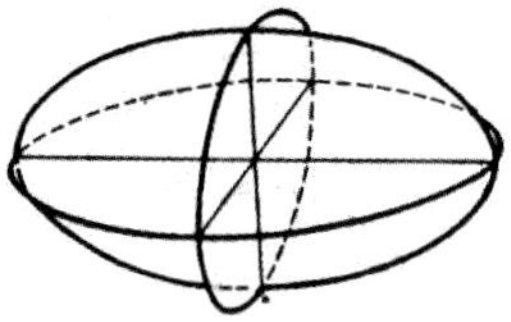

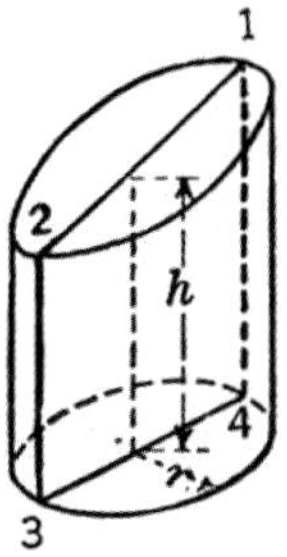

Na
(1.86)

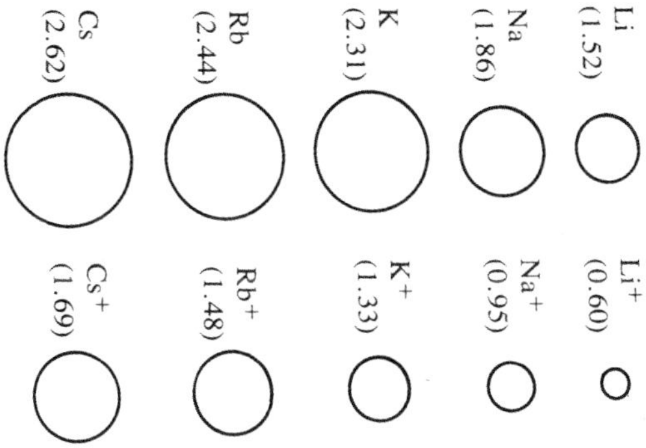

K
(2.31)

Rb
(2.44)

Cs
(2.62)

Li+
(0.60)

Na+
(0.95)

K+
(1.33)

Rb+
(1.48)

Cs+
(1.69)

1

2

3

4

h

r

D

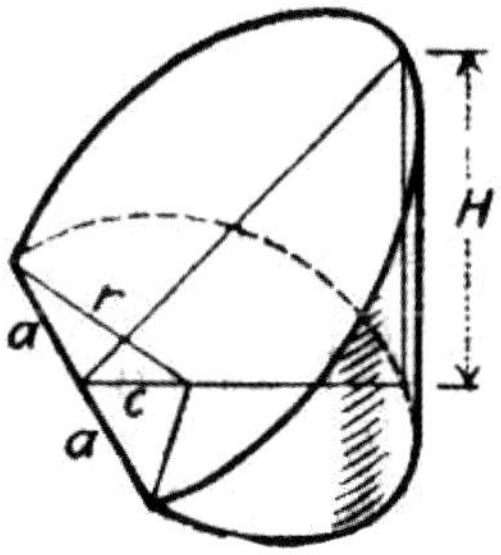

C

A

B

O

H

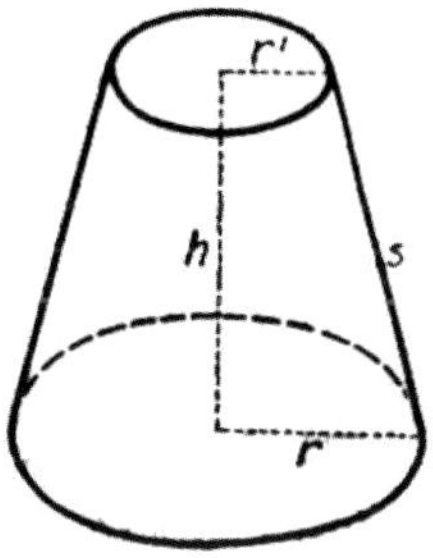

r

a

a

c

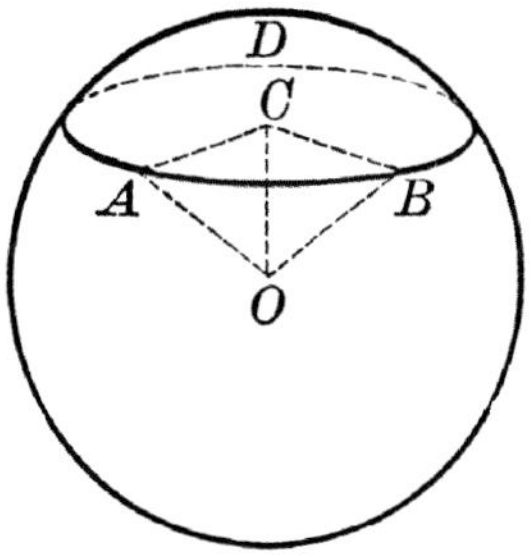

r'

h

s

r

θ

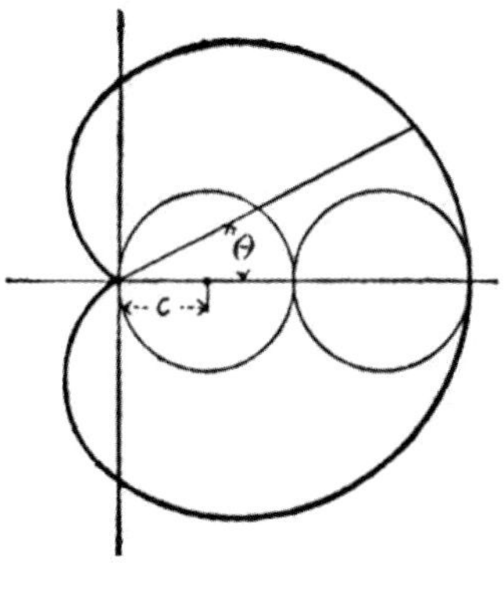

c

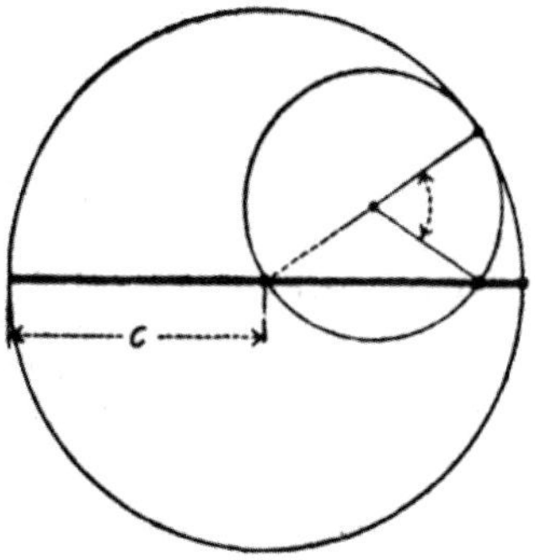

c

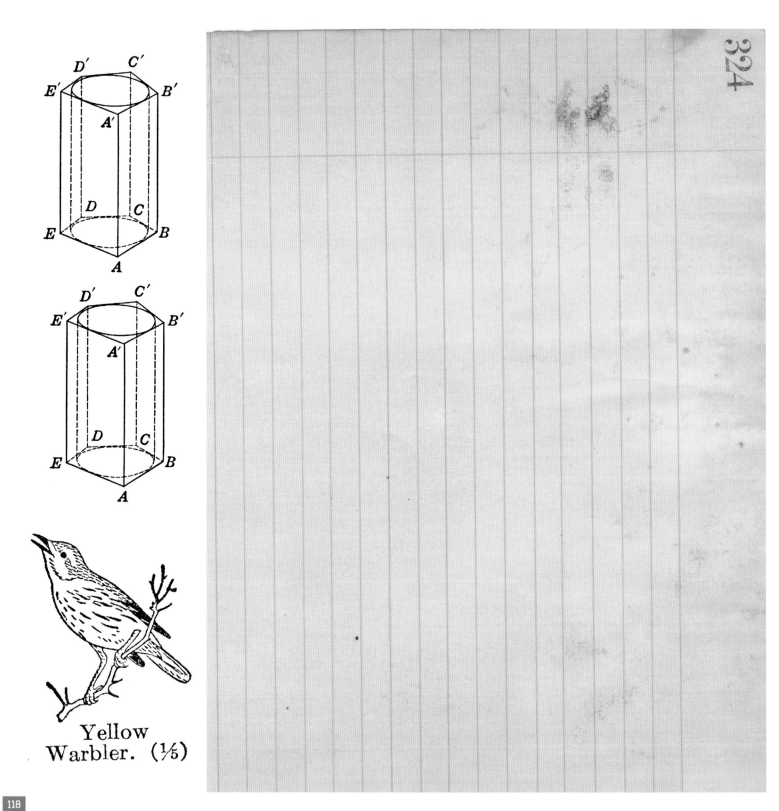

Yellow
Warbler. (⅕)

Address _____

Office or
Department _____

_____ Number _____

	U. S. Bonds	With-holding Tax	Hospitali-zation	Insur-ance	State Income Tax					Total Deduc-tions	NET PAY ROLL AMOUNT	
												1st Qtr.
												2nd Qtr.
												Total 6 Mos.
												3rd Qtr.
												Total 9 Mos.
												4th Qtr.
												Total for Year

D E D U C T I O N S

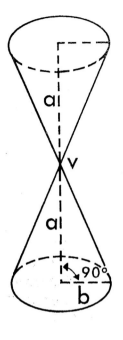

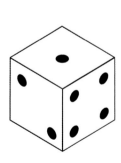

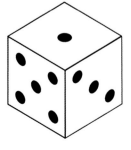

9th Week
1st Term
1891.

Oakley Apr. 25, 1891

268th regular meeting Oakley Building and Loan Co. called to order by Pres. Remke.

Roll of officers called and absentees noted. The minutes of Apr. 18, were read and approved.

The Attorney presented another report on the title of Mrs. Ella Barr, which was received and recorded in the book of Attorney's Reports.

On motion an order was drawn in favor of Mr. H. P. Sabbert for $3.13 and charged to the Expense Acct.

The Attorney presented a report on the title of Louise Hegeney, which was accepted and filed.

The Appraising Committee's report on the same property, was read and accepted.

A vote was then taken on the security offered for the loan, and it was accepted by 7 Yeas.

It was then moved to draw an order in favor of Mrs. Louise Hegeney for $1750, and place the same in the hands of the president till the mortgage is ready for record. This was adopted.

On motion an order was drawn in favor of Henry Rohs, Book 10, for $1453.85

Also an order in favor of Wm. Holdt for $614.00 — Book 85

Receipts

I love your verses with all my heart, dear
Miss Barrett, — and this is no off-hand com-
plimentary letter that I shall write, whatever
else, no prompt matter-of-course recognition
of your genius and there a graceful and natu-
ral end of the thing: since the day last week
when I first read your poems, I quite laugh
to remember how I have been turning and
turning again in my mind what I should
be able to tell you of their effect upon me
for in the first flush of delight I thought
I would this once get out of my habit of
purely passive enjoyment, when I do really
enjoy, and thoroughly justify my admi-
ration — perhaps even, as a loyal fellow-
craftsman should, try and find fault and
do you some little good to be proud of
hereafter! — but nothing comes of it

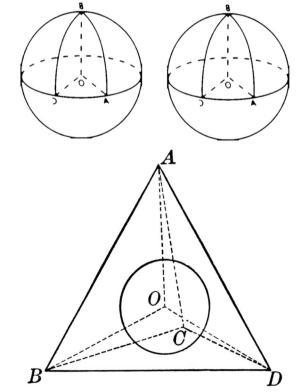

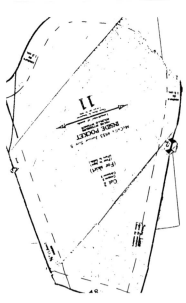

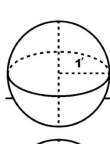

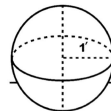

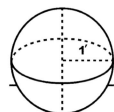

Reducing Specialist Says:

LOSE WEIGHT

MOST ANY PART OF THE BODY WITH

Spot Reducer

Relaxing · Soothing · Penetrating Massage

REDUCE

Where It Shows Most

handcuff

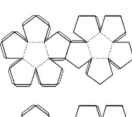

handcuff

DON'T TAKE CHANCES !

GET FREE PLAN

MAIL COUPON!

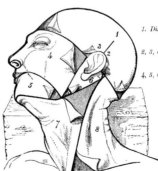

1. Dissection of scalp.

2, 3, of auricular region.

4, 5, 6, of face.

7, 8, of neck.

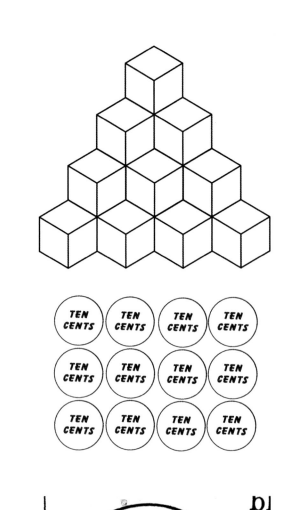

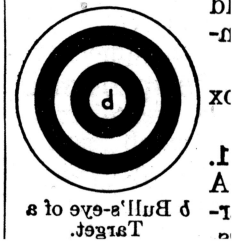

b Bull's-eye of a Target.

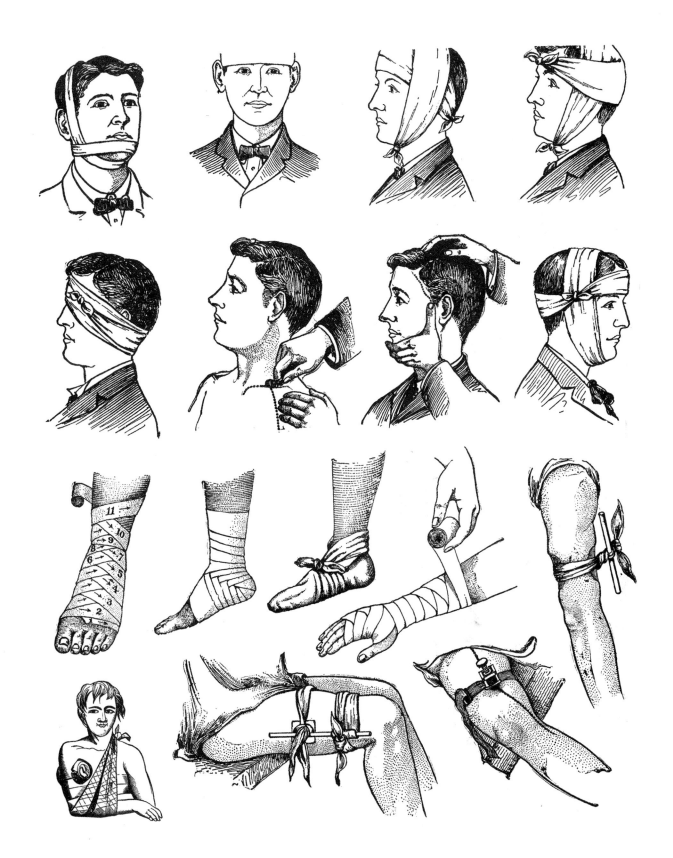

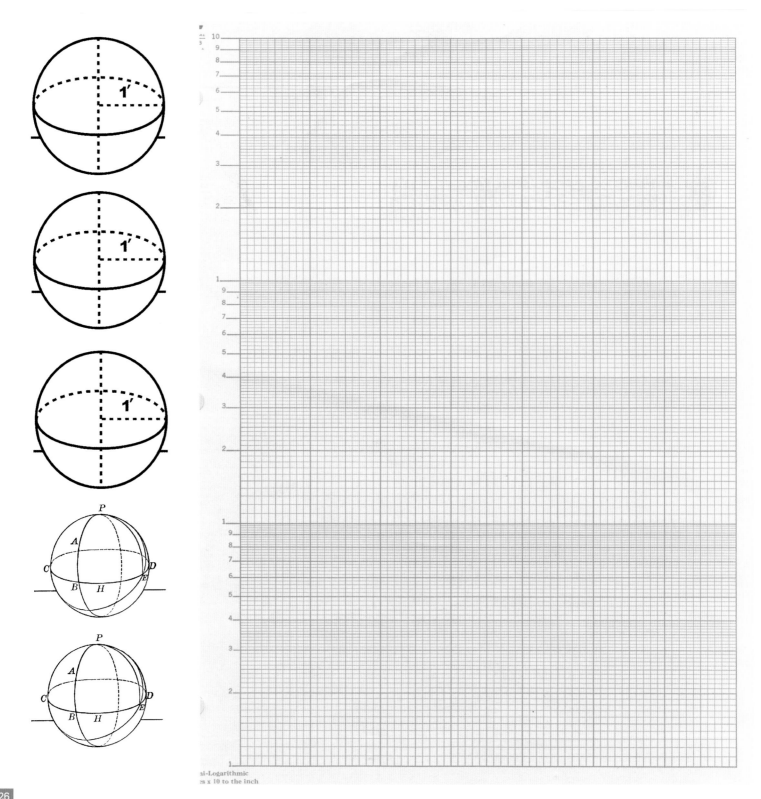

ni-Logarithmic
es x 10 to the inch

Redwing, l. (N)

J

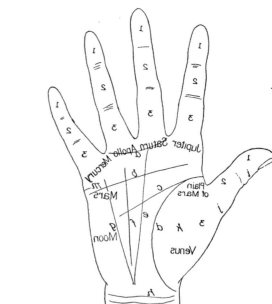

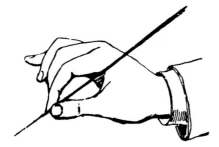

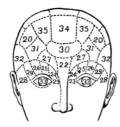

THE HAND IN PALMISTRY

(a) Ring of Venus   (g) Line of health
(b) Bracelets   (h) Line of heart
(c) Will   (c) Line of head
(f) Reason   (d) Line of life

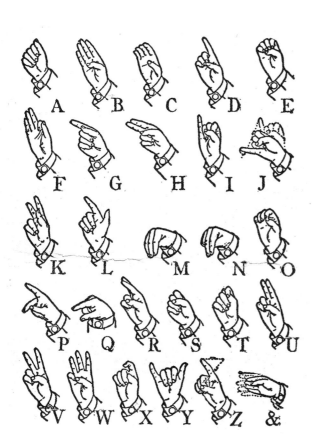

A   B   C   D   E
F   G   H   I   J
K   L   M   N   O
P   Q   R   S   T   U
V   W   X   Y   Z   &

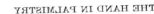

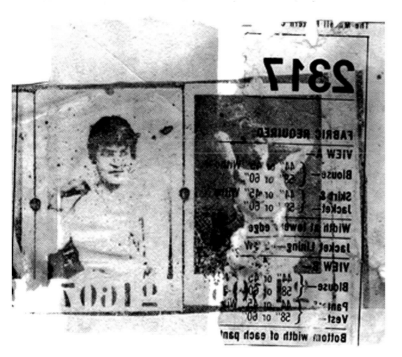

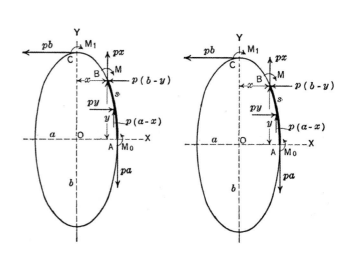

RESOURCES

GLUES

www.ganebrothers.com

www.hollanders.com

www.plaidonline.com

www.talasonline.com

SCISSORS

www3.fiskars.com

MAT BOARD

www.bdmatboard.com

www.crescentcardboard.com/matboard.html

MAT CUTTERS

www.logangraphic.com

ACRYLIC MEDIUMS

www.goldenpaints.com/products/medsadds/index.php

www.liquitex.com/Mediums

STORAGE BAGS

www.clearbags.com

www.lightimpressionsdirect.com

SUPPORTS

www.danielsmith.com

www.dickblick.com

www.utrechtart.com

IMAGE-EDITING SOFTWARE

www.adobe.com

www.gimp.org

http://picasa.google.com

IMAGERY

See the links in the imagery section on page 21.

BOOKS

Blom, Ina. *Ray Johnson: Please Add to & Return.* Barcelona: Museu D'Art Contemporani de Barcelona, 2010.

Brommer, Gerald. *Collage Techniques: A Guide for Artists and Illustrators.* New York: Watson-Guptill, 1994.

Cotter, Holland. *Lenore Tawney: Signs on the Wind: Postcard Collages.* Petaluma, CA: Pomegranate Communications, 2002.

Fine, Ruth. *The Art of Romare Bearden.* New York: Harry N. Abrams, 2003.

Kotz, Mary Lynn. *Rauschenberg: Art and Life.* New York: Harry N. Abrams, 2004.

Lark Books. *Masters: Collage: Major Works by Leading Artists.* Asheville, NC: Lark Crafts, 2010.

Lidwell, William. *Universal Principles of Design.* Beverly, MA: Rockport Publishers, 2003.

Luyken, Gunda. *Hannah Höch: Picture Book.* Berlin: The Green Box, 2010.

Schulz, Isabel. *Kurt Schwitters: Color and Collage.* Houston, TX: The Menil Collection, 2010.

Taylor, Brandon. *Collage: The Making of Modern Art.* London: Thames & Hudson, 2006.

Waldman, Diane. *Joseph Cornell: Master of Dreams.* New York: Harry N. Abrams, 2006.

Wong, Wucius. *Principles of Two-Dimensional Design.* Hoboken, NJ: Wiley, 1972.

DVDS

The Art of Romare Bearden. Homevision, 2004.

The Gleaners and I. Zeitgeist Films, 2002.

How to Draw a Bunny. Palm Pictures, 2004.

ABOUT THE AUTHOR

Randel Plowman graduated from Northern Kentucky University with a BFA in printmaking. He has worked in collage since 1982, and his art has been exhibited in solo and juried exhibitions throughout the United States; in addition, his pieces have appeared in many public and private collections in North America and abroad, including the Cincinnati Art Museum. Plowman's work has been cited in numerous publications, including the *New York Times* and *USA Today*; featured in *How Design* magazine, *Artist* magazine, and *Somerset Studio* magazine; and used as cover art on numerous books. He curated *Masters: Collage*, a book featuring the work of more than 40 contemporary collage artists, for Lark Crafts. He also teaches workshops in printmaking and collage and has a popular collage blog at www.acollageaday.com and website at www.randelplowman.com. He currently lives and works in Madison, Wisconsin, where he is pursuing an MFA at the University of Wisconsin-Madison.

ACKNOWLEDGMENTS

This book would not have been possible without the help of many wonderful and creative people. I would like to thank:

Stacy Blint, Ron Isaacs and Andrea Knarr for their support and guidance.

All the fans and collectors who continue to visit my blog and support my work.

I also owe a debt of gratitude to all the wonderful people at Lark Crafts for helping me publish this book.

A special thanks goes out to my editor, Kathleen McCafferty, for guiding me through the process of completing this book. You were wonderful to work with.

I would also like to thank Travis Medford for his great design sensibility.

INDEX